"A thoughtful book that substitutes substance for conventional customer service hype. It all starts with turning on your internal customers—creating a true customer-driven culture in your organization. He tells you how to do it and how to measure it."

—Davis Young, President and Chief Operating Officer,
Edward Howard & Co.
and author of *Building Your Company's Good Name*

"Provides a unique packaging of Massnick's experience as an executive directing customer satisfaction and persuasion activities for major corporations. In a series of well-crafted chapters, he deals with current approaches to customer satisfaction and provides a revealing look at how functional units need to operate in a customer-centered organization. The book combines a valuable vision and a prescription."

—Robert A. Schwarz, President, Total Quality Systems

"This book hits the bull's eye dead center. It is full of ideas that every CEO should be thinking about, I found it so important, and so directly related to the concerns that I have, that I am reading it for a second time—slowly and carefully."

—Ernie Schroeder, CEO, Schroeder Milk Company

"Massnick's approach to customer satisfaction is systemic, and his message is loud and clear: To truly satisfy the customer, ALL functions of an organization must collaborate. The process of optimal customer satisfaction is organic, and needs to be understood and operationalized accordingly. Failure to understand this concept is a set-up for eventual business suicide."

—Bernard Saunders, President, Integra Learning Systems
and co-author of *Ten Steps to a Learning Organization*

"Being in the survey research business, I was impressed with the clarity of the ideas expressed on customer satisfaction measurement. But even more important were the ideas about cultural change, training, and the way 'focus on the customer' fits in with concepts about learning organizations. I intend to make this book the basis of a training program for our people."

—Jack Semler, CEO, Readex Corporation

"Fills a void that has not been addressed until now. With sound research, excellent writing, and perspective conclusions, Massnick has produced a book that can make a significant difference as American business struggles with shifting paradigms. Leaders who are in the midst of epochal change often find it difficult to see and understand the big picture. This book definitely helps."

—Terry Hitchcock, Ph.D., consultant and past CEO of major companies
author of *American Business: The Last Hurrah*

"For those caught up in the maelstrom of change that is today's workplace, Forler Massnick is extending a helping hand. He makes a compelling case for a new way of doing business, recognizing and honoring customers, first and foremost. His formula is a lot different from the way most companies function today. It is a must-read for executives who want to stay on the bucking bronco of today's business world."

—Mary Regnier, President
Transformational Resources International

"Forler Massnick is one of the wisest people I have ever met in the world of business and that wisdom comes through abundantly in this book."

—Bryan Mattimore, author of *99% Inspiration*
and Contributing Editor to *Success Magazine*

"Massnick takes a provocative look at the very essence of the Total Quality movement—how to add value to the customer by continuously improving the company's products and services in terms of defect prevention, cycle time improvement, and lower costs. Massnick emphasizes the fact that 'value' is defined by the customer and that working towards customer satisfaction needs to be the top priority of every employee in the company. Read this book and begin to understand what it takes to really serve your customer."

—Tim Krieg, Executive Vice President, Quality and Human Resources
FSI® International, Inc.

# THE CUSTOMER IS CEO

## How to Measure What Your Customers Want—And Make Sure They Get It

### Forler Massnick

**amacom**

American Management Association

New York . Atlanta . Boston . Chicago . Kansas City . San Francisco . Washington, D. C.
Brussels . Mexico City . Tokyo . Toronto

**Library of Congress Cataloging-in-Publication Data**

Massnick, Forler.
    The customer is CEO : how to measure what your customers want—and
make sure they get it / Forler Massnick.
        p.   cm.
    Includes bibliographical references and index.
    ISBN 0-8144-0346-8
    1. Customer services—United States.   2. Consumer satisfaction—
United States.   I. Title.
HF5415.5.M174   1997
658.8'12—dc21                                                     96-53589
                                                                        CIP

Printing number

10 9 8 7 6 5 4 3 2 1

To my wife,
**Carrie,**
whose love, spirituality, wisdom, and
balance are a constant source of inspiration,
encouragement, comfort, stability—and joy.

# Contents

# Acknowledgments

In attempting to acknowledge the sources for the information and ideas that make up the messages in this book, I feel like the actor who began an award acceptance speech by saying, "I want to thank everyone I've ever met."

I will be more specific in identifying some of the people to whom I owe a special debt of gratitude. Jack Semler, a long time client—one of the best a consultant could hope for—who first challenged me to learn everything I could about customer satisfaction. Everett Dale and Norm Schmitt, two grizzled veterans of the quality wars, who provided continuous wise counsel while generously sharing long lifetimes of experience. Bob Schwarz, who got me heavily involved in the American Society for Quality Control, an experience from which I have benefitted greatly. Mary Regnier, an inspired leader and teacher concerning the esoterica of transformation in the world of work, who helps make sense out of it all. A person I have never met, yet whose writings have influenced me profoundly, Peter Drucker.

Finally I owe a debt of gratitude to all of the bosses I have had over the years. Some have been superb role models, mentors, leaders, and friends. Others haven't been. Nonetheless they have all contributed to my knowledge, skills, experience base, and any wisdom I may have acquired over time.

# Prologue
# A Moment of
# Truth at Mega
# Motors

The first hint of daylight could be seen on the horizon as the cars with their headlights blazing pulled into the executive garage, marking the exceptionally early arrival of the members of the operating committee of Mega Motors, Inc., the giant automobile company.

Jaws were set and the pace was a bit more brisk than usual as one by one the executives strode across the spotless floor of the garage and entered the building. Several glanced at their watches as they went directly to the boardroom. They assumed their accustomed places at the huge gleaming table, as big as the deck of an aircraft carrier.

At precisely 7:00 A.M., the chairman entered the room and took his seat at the head of the table. His familiar affable manner and engaging smile appeared to have taken a leave of absence. He nodded to the assembly but didn't speak. Instead he pushed a button, and the curtains covering the screen behind him parted.

A colorful chart revealed the most recent sales figures for the company's heavily advertised, much-heralded new model. The numbers were shockingly low. Then a succession of charts and graphs appeared on the screen. Each stayed up just long enough to be understood and then dissolved to the next.

There was no need for explanation. It was distressingly apparent that the new model was not selling well in any region, not faring well against the competition, and not even within hailing distance of forecasts. The company had gambled billions—and apparently rolled snake eyes.

The screen went blank and the curtain silently covered it. The chairman leaned forward, wordlessly scanning the faces in front of him. After an awkward pause, he said solemnly, "I have only one question. How could we have been so wrong?"

The executives shifted uneasily in their chairs. No one volunteered to speak up. When the silence became painful, the chairman suddenly stood up and began pacing. "Look," he said, "we're all in this together. We all have some degree of responsibility, and we're all paid well enough to have some ideas. Now, I'm going to go around the table and call on each of you. I want you to tell us what you really think, with no holds barred. There are some simple ground rules: No excuses. No defending the past. No personal criticisms."

The chairman sat down and turned to the chief financial officer, at his right. "Let's start with you," he said.

She leaned forward, smiling tentatively. "From what I have been able to determine, the problem seems to be the price. People like the cars; not much question about that. But they are either unwilling or unable to pay over twenty-five thousand dollars for a car in the class they perceive this to be in. We priced it the way we have always priced new models, but I guess we have finally hit the stops. It's sticker shock all over again. The last time sticker shock hit the market, at least our competition was doing the same things we were. This time we're kind of hanging out there by ourselves. Frankly, we need better ways of measuring how people feel about prices. If that's going to be a key factor in pricing, then we need to take it into account right at the start when we begin developing new models. There is not much point in giving people all of the features they say they want if they're not willing to pay for them."

Beside her sat the controller, a young man with a Wharton degree and ambitions to be the next CFO. "I'm glad she mentioned measurement," he intoned. "We need better ways of measuring what's going to happen. When you think about it, the financial measurements that we're all accustomed to are lagging indicators. They're basically historical. The sales figures that we've just seen are the result of decisions made years ago when we began developing the cars we're now sell-ing—or perhaps more accurately, trying to sell. Sales, profits, return on investment, cash flow, value added . . . they're all just score-keeping for a game that's already over. We need to do a better job of measuring what our customers are thinking and feeling, what our dealers are experiencing, and what we're getting complaints about. If we had done this effectively, we wouldn't have gotten blind-sided."

It was the marketing vice president's turn. "We talk a lot about customer satisfaction being the driving force of this company, but is it really? I think we've got to take a good, hard look at ourselves. And I mean the people around this table. Be honest now: If I ask you in secret what's the biggest concern you have in your job every day, how many of you would say it's figuring out how to satisfy customers? Most of you would probably say it was profits, or market share, or cutting expense . . . maybe even keeping your job, surviving. I don't want to sound cynical, but isn't it hypocritical for us to say the company is customer-driven and ask everybody else in the company to carry out their jobs that way when we as leaders are behaving quite differently? If we were really concerned about customers, we'd know enough about them to not be producing products they won't buy."

Then came the head of domestic sales, with his deep radio voice. "I remember learning about a market research study done by a car company—not this one—in the fifties. People with clipboards were sent out all over the country to knock on doors and ask homeowners what they wanted in a car. Most people said they wanted good, basic transportation. No frills. Good mileage. Sensible cars. The company started making cars like that, and it almost went out of business. No-body bought. It turned out that people just wanted to look good for the interviewers—you know, solid and sensible. The researchers caught on and tried again. This time, they asked people what they thought their *neighbors* wanted in a car. Without the need to impress the interviewers, people revealed what they themselves really wanted. Suddenly, it was flashy cars with lots of horsepower, options, luxury features, and so on. The reality is that people will lie, say one thing and do another. Is it possible that our market research people aren't taking this into consideration?"

The vice president of engineering spoke next. "That's an interest-ing point about how misleading surveys can be. As a matter of fact, every source we have for information about customers has limitations or flaws. I've come to the conclusion that the only way to get at the truth, or come anywhere near it, is to have lots of sources of informa-tion, and then cross-check the data. I don't think we're doing that very well, at least not from the reports I see. Lots of information is getting pigeon-holed or dead-ended. For example, product complaints that come into the sales department aren't getting to the product designers who could do something about it. Apropos of the points made earlier about financial information, we have good systems and processes for crunching financial numbers, but nothing comparable to deal with customer-satisfaction data."

The only other woman at the table, the brilliant vice president of advertising, said, "Timing is everything. If we had put this new model on the market a couple of years ago, we wouldn't be having this meeting. It would have been gangbusters. But it took us four years. I think we sensed the market all right; we just missed it. We need to figure out how to react faster. For heaven's sake, we won World War II in four years. You'd think designing a car might take a little less time than that. I agree with what's been said about getting better information on our customers, but it won't do us much good if we can't react to it a lot better than we have."

The avuncular vice president of human resources was next. He cleared his throat, looked over his half-glasses, and spoke authoritatively. "In one way or another, everyone has been talking about the importance of getting closer to our customers. If that is what we want to do, in fact have to do, and I'm all for it, we're going to have to put our money where our mouth is. By that I mean we are going to have to find ways to link customer satisfaction and compensation and recognition. Putting it simply, if we want our people doing a better job of relating to customers then we should be rewarding those who do it well. We do that now for improving financial performance. People are pretty smart. It doesn't take them long to figure out what really matters."

The vice president of administration chimed in, "Let's not overlook the fact that there is no way we can do all these wonderful things about relating to customers unless our own people are happy in their jobs. That brings up the subject of internal customer satisfaction. Only a relatively small percentage of our people have contact with outside customers, but everybody is responding to the needs of somebody else in the company. Let's make sure we measure internal customer satisfaction, and reward and recognize people for excelling at that too. What does this have to do with the original question, how could we have been so wrong? A lot, I believe. Business is people, and, frankly, I don't think our people have a clear vision of the kind of company we want to be."

All eyes turned to the respected vice president of quality whose turn had come. "For the past fifteen years or so we've been hammering on quality. It was necessary and right. And we've been successful, but so has everybody else in the business. We're at parity. Everybody is producing low-defect products. The problem is we've lost sight of one of the basic principles of the quality movement. Quality is not decided by some statistical process control chart. The customer decides what quality is. While we're doing a great job on product, something like eighty percent of the dissatisfaction voiced by customers has nothing to do with product. It has to do with service, attitudes, relationships—the human aspects of doing business. I submit, if we were doing a good job of attacking our eighty percent problem, we wouldn't be having the kind of problem we are having today."

The last person to be heard from was the head of North American operations, a veteran of plant operations respected as a real car man. He looked the part—square-jawed, ham-fisted. "You might be surprised to hear me say what I'm going to say," he began. "We're still running things around here the way it was when Henry Ford, Alfred Sloan, and Walter Chrysler were the movers and shakers. We're about as receptive to change as Mt. Rushmore. When we grew up in the industry, the public pretty much took whatever we gave them, and liked it. Those days are gone forever. People have choices. They want it fast, they want it right. They want value delivered with a smile. And you know what, somebody is going to give it to them. Ladies and gentlemen, if we don't get off our hind ends and be that someone, we're going to be history."

The words were greeted with a tomb-like silence. All eyes turned to the chairman. The anticipation was palpable. Unexpectedly the hint of a smile crept over his countenance. There was a dramatic pause before he spoke. "Now we're getting somewhere," he said softly. "I started out by saying I had only one question, how could we have been so wrong? I now have another question. I don't expect or want an answer today, but I want you to think about it. A lot of what we heard today, we were hearing for the first time. Why? For heaven's sake, why?"

# Introduction

If you occupy a leadership position in an organization, any kind of organization, and you are not sure where to find the answers to the problems that bedevil you, look no further. This book is written for you. After all of the buzzwords have buzzed off, there is a truth you can rely on to get you safely through the turbulent waters of a world under deluge.

This is not a textbook, a handbook, or a manual. It's written for busy executives and managers who don't have the time or inclination to slog through a tome. It's for readers who respond to entertainingly presented ideas that are to the point, readers impatient with pedantry and scholarship.

Some of the most powerful, impactful ideas in recorded history are elegant and simple.

The United States of America was founded on the idea of government *of the people, by the people, and for the people.*

*Kill or be killed*, the rule of the jungle, has been replaced by *a society of laws.*

*Do unto others as you would have others do unto you.* Virtually every religion has some version of that Golden Rule.

*Satisfaction guaranteed or your money back.* The Sears, Roebuck Company revolutionized merchandising around 1900 with an idea stated so simply everybody could understand it. Clear, unequivocal, simple.

*All men are created equal.*

## A Simple Idea With Far-Reaching Implications

This book is about an idea so stunningly obvious that when first mentioned it is more likely to produce yawns than ah-ha's.

## The Customer Is the Chief Executive Officer
## C = CEO

*Customer* means the recipient of any kind of product or service provided by an organization, a recipient inside or outside. *CEO* means the leader of any kind of organization: business, nonprofit, or governmental.

Am I saying that customers perform the functions of a CEO? Yes, exactly. And organizations that recognize this can transform themselves to be healthier and more successful.

If you are a CEO, don't mutter that I shouldn't let the door hit me in the rear on my way out. I'm not advocating the elimination of your job. Read on, and be patient, please.

If you're not a CEO, if you love and admire your CEO, or if you dislike and obsess about the person at the pinnacle, neither am I suggesting that we spring a trap in the front office. I'm saying only that the real power factor in the equation above, the customer, be honored. To find out what this means, please also be patient and read on.

# CEOs Are Responsible for Providing Leadership

First, the basics. Few would argue with the concept that the fundamental responsibility of the CEO is to provide leadership that results in success. Couple that with what Jack Smith, CEO of General Motors, said: "Focus everything—all assets, all decisions—on your customers. They are the ultimate arbiters of success or failure."

It is exquisitely simple when you think about it. Organizations need money to survive (to say nothing of thrive). The money comes as a result of decisions made by customers. So who ultimately is in charge?

What organization do you know that devotes more than lip service to this starkly simple reality? But rather than "read their lips," watch what they do. Despite protestations to the contrary, most organizations are predominantly internally focused and have only superficial knowledge of the wants and needs of their customers.

That's a tough statement. This book supports the statement with evidence, contrasting what an organization looks like when it acknowledges the rightful role of the customer as CEO. This book also shows, incidentally, how much more fulfilling and pleasant life can be for people occupying the CEO's hot seat in today's world of bewildering, pell-mell change.

The message to CEOs: Move over a bit and make room for the customer. You will only gain, not lose.

The message to everyone else: Recognize who your real boss is—the customer—and act accordingly. And don't forget that you, too, are a customer; exult in the power and use it wisely.

The decisions and actions of CEOs, past and present, permeate the organizations they head. If the customer is to move figuratively into the corner office on Mahogany Row, the impact has to be felt everywhere in the organization.

## What a Customer-Centered Organization Will Look Like

This book is organized to show—function by function, department by department—what a customer-centered organization will look like. I choose the future tense deliberately here. While there are a number of organizations that have excelled by paying attention to customers (many are cited as examples throughout the book), I know of no company that has fully attained the ideal of C = CEO.

It is also difficult if not impossible to "piecemeal" your way to customer-centeredness. It requires a distinct, and in many ways difficult, shift in thinking. The overused term *paradigm shift* is difficult to avoid, but it's precisely what is needed.

Legions of managers devote entire dreary careers to adjusting the minutiae of their work—trifling with the trivia. Such busywork obscures fundamental problems that are recognized in the questions "What business are we in? Why are we in it?"

Organizations with deep roots into a hierarchical past, and managers steeped in the old ideas of how people should function at work, cannot escape change by trifling with trivia. Band-Aid programs have no staying power, and when people revert it is usually to a failing status quo. By directing the dialogue to a broad focus, simply stated in a way everyone can understand, seemingly complex issues fall into place.

This book is about changing the dialogue, no matter what your business or organization, to center on a simple concept: *Your purpose is to serve customers who have the power to determine whether you are successful.*

The most important strategic decision any organization can make is to let the customer rule the roost. Yet few have done it. I hear executives talking all the time about customer satisfaction, about their organizations being customer-driven or customer-centered. Some even go so far as to say they intend to *delight* their customers. Customer satisfaction has been trivialized by people who don't understand it.

## The Curse of Customer Satisfaction

The curse is that customer satisfaction is easy to talk about. Who can argue with the idea? It makes wonderful boilerplate for executive speeches and annual reports. On the surface, customer satisfaction seems relatively simple to accomplish. Take a few surveys. Train people to be courteous. Go the extra mile every now and then.

In organizations where the thinking runs deeper, executives soon discover that a commitment to being customer-driven has the potential to change everything, absolutely everything. Few organizations have demonstrated their willingness to do that. Instead they shy away, choosing to do business as usual behind a veneer of customer satisfaction.

The destiny of the timid is mediocrity. When the peripatetic George Plimpton set out to discover the difference between merely very good athletes and those who elevate themselves a step higher to achieve world-class standing, he identified what he called the $x$ factor: the ability to focus intensely, without distraction, on what you want to achieve.

There is an $x$ factor in business too. Organizations that are clear on what their driving force is, and that stay focused on it with laser-like intensity, become world-class. Those that flit about, hummingbirdlike, from bloom to bloom dissipate their energy and never achieve distinction.

This book explores what customer satisfaction really means as a driving force in an organization. It enables readers to play with a full deck when making decisions about the role of the customer in their organization. For those whom it emboldens, this book offers an opportunity to move ahead of the competition and command the dominance enjoyed by leaders.

The first six chapters deal with the kinds of issues that occupy and perplex senior executives: crafting a compelling vision for the organization, fostering a culture that makes the vision real, surviving and benefiting from the uncertainty of change, adapting organizational structures to fit new concepts of doing business, and communicating through a clearly stated strategic plan.

You've probably seen business bookshelves lined with self-help treatises on how to do all of these things. Many of the concepts have literally become movements with devoted followers. Chapters 7 through 12 cover the how-to consequences of customer satisfaction as it relates to those movements.

## Every Functional Department Is Affected

The basic thesis of this book is that there cannot be a truly customer-centered organization unless the impact of the concept is felt in every functional department. Chapters 13 through 17 get down to cases on what needs to happen with regard to your people (human resources/ personnel), finance, marketing, product development, and customer service.

Chapters 18 through 22 discuss in detail how to apply the tools of customer satisfaction. The essential nature of measurement is described. The tricky subject of defining who the customer is gets attention. How to avoid misunderstanding and misusing surveys is explained. The advisability of linking customer satisfaction and employee compensation is explored, as is the crucial role of the often-overlooked production and operations people.

Finally, in the addendum are valuable resource documents and tools that are needed to support customer-satisfaction initiatives: W. Edwards Deming's Fourteen Points and his Seven Deadly Diseases, a summary of the Malcolm Baldrige National Quality Award criteria, information on ISO 9000, sample survey questionnaires, and steps toward implementing an employee suggestion system.

The balance of this introduction is written for busy leaders who like to work from executive summaries. It is a capsule of the book's main points, by chapter.

## Vision

There is no more powerful force to drive an organization than a vision. But to succeed it must be attractive, worthwhile, achievable, and widely shared. The vision of an organization as being truly customer-centered meets all of the standards for a viable vision, but only if leaders understand fully what that means to the organization. There are disciplines that can be applied to help determine whether a vision is "right." Once a vision has been articulated, it is up to the leaders to set personal examples for the organization through their own conduct.

## Culture

There is a way of thinking about things and a way of doing things in every organization; together they constitute its culture. As influencers of the culture, leaders need to examine their priorities, the time spent reinforcing corporate values, and how effectively they are demonstrating by their actions a commitment to the customer. Companies that stress shareholder value as the primary driver of their culture are making a mistake (as we see immediately in Chapter 1). A more balanced view of the role of the corporation in society calls for elevating the importance of customers.

## Change

How do you get people to participate in something they don't like (change) because the survival of the organization depends on it? Uncertain of the outcome of change initiatives that could affect them, people employ a variety of tactics, conscious and subconscious, to slow things down. There is a clear-cut, simple way to create an environment for turned-on, committed, responsible employees: Get everyone in the organization focused on serving customers, internal or external. When that becomes an obsession, resistance to change melts away.

## Organization

Like it or not, we live in a time of epochal change. This is a time when leaders must be a party to the dismantling of the system that bred them—as distasteful and unsettling as that task may be. Introducing customer satisfaction as the true driving force of an organization can be accomplished only if the shock waves to the organization are anticipated and welcomed. Each functional area erects its own barriers to customer satisfaction. An organization must be carefully designed if it is to use customer-satisfaction measurement as its nervous system, an approach recommended in Chapter 1, "Measurement Magic."

## Strategic Planning

Various approaches to strategic planning have moved in and out of favor in the executive suite. Technology forecasting, market research, scenario planning, and competitor analysis have all had their day. Now the emphasis is on "reconceiving" the corporation and the industries in which it competes in order to anticipate the future. Strategic planners need validity checks on the information they work with. Market research data should be compared to what trained listeners are hearing. An effective customer-satisfaction measurement system, which can be described as "organizational telemetry," brings in information from multiple sources. Validating and analyzing the information leads to balanced conclusions amenable to action.

## Quality

The simple idea at the heart of the quality movement—the customer decides what quality is—represents both a boon and a barrier. The quality idea got management's attention first, and customer satisfaction slipped in behind it. Unfortunately, because quality is often perceived as a project with a beginning and an end, that can happen to customer satisfaction too. Many organizations pursue quality within the framework of their bureaucracies, instead of by listening to customers.

## Reengineering

Many companies have simply reengineered systems that shouldn't exist at all; or they have made wonderful improvements in productivity, but for products or services that the market no longer wants or soon will not. If reengineering means starting with a clean slate, one of the first things that needs to be written on the slate is an accurate description of customer expectations, described now and into the future to the extent they can be demystified. To start with anything else is folly.

## Learning Organization

The conventional wisdom is that perhaps the only remaining area where lasting competitive advantage can be achieved is in the ability of people in organizations to learn. Very practical business considerations are producing a rethinking of what training and learning are all about. The most effective adult learning model is self-directed learning. For people to sustain motivation to learn and grow, the process has to make sense to them. To supplant dependence on a teacher or boss, people need goals they can identify with. A commitment to serve customers, internal or external, and measurement that shows how well that goal is being met can provide the impetus for continuous learning.

## Teams

There are parallels between the concept of teams as an effective organizational technique and Total Quality Management. It is hard to find fault with either idea, yet the organizational landscape is littered with failed programs in both areas that started out with the best of intentions. There is a distinction between *real* teams and groups that management *calls* teams. At the very least, the team needs (1) to know what the end product of its work should be and (2) effective leaders. When team leaders position themselves as representing the interest of customers, the customer can become their badge of authority. Wise leaders recognize that the traditional, hierarchical style of management is antithetical to teams.

## Leadership

For an organization to become customer-centered, it must have strong leadership. The first and perhaps greatest challenge facing leaders shifting to a customer focus is to personally accept the idea that everything will be different—especially the way they spend their time and conduct themselves. Faced with the idea of making a basic, far-reaching decision, many executives take cover in incrementalism—which is a formula for failure. Value creator individuals, on the other hand, are constantly stirring things up, trying new ideas, taking risks, stimulating change.

## Your People

A top priority for organizations that are serious about customer satisfaction must be the attitudes and feelings of their own people. An organization of people who are unhappy in their work is incapable of satisfying customers. Management by slogan doesn't work. In order to get buy-in at all levels of an organization, a vision must be not only announced but explained and supported by policies and procedures. Until goals, objectives, and personal aspirations are aligned, there is only noise.

## Finance

An enlightened finance department is the nerve center of an organization, including customer satisfaction measurement. Finance people are trained in statistics and information systems, the building blocks of customer satisfaction measurement. It is within the power of any organization to set up measuring systems that turn static accounting numbers into something more like moving holograms with color and sound. Peter Drucker says, "There is only one valid definition of business purpose: *to create a customer.*"

## Marketing

Marketing as it has been taught and practiced in the postwar period has been *mass* marketing, an idea whose time is passing. The marketing of the future considers people as individuals, not as faceless, mass-migrating lemmings. This altered perspective changes all of the rules. Customers are demanding the world, and if you don't give it to them someone else will. The rallying cry for the future in marketing circles is likely to be *customer retention*. Companies are beginning to accept these precepts: Service is more important than products; the old idea of a vendor is passé; it is necessary to live the life of your customer; employees are not disposable.

## Product Development

There are two reasons why companies have difficulty with new product development. Virtually every department of a company is affected by or involved in some way with new products, yet communications between departments is abysmal. And secondly, the voice of the customer is seldom heard loudly and clearly by all of the people involved in product-development decision making. When organizations make a determined effort to become customer-centered and work hard at the cultural change that is incumbent upon that decision, the issues that block effective new product development tend to dissolve.

## Customer Service

Instead of treating customer service as a low-level, low-budget function, leaders should carefully craft customer service strategies, considering such issues as the optimal mix and level of service for various customers. At the heart of the idea (which is in fact a necessity) of developing a customer service strategy is the need for a valid, consistent, comprehensive customer satisfaction measurement system. The alternative is management by intuition, not management by fact, the concept stressed by quality experts.

## Measurement

Basic to any serious strategy of customer satisfaction is the need for measurement. An effective system, I've already suggested, can be thought of as organizational telemetry. The elements of such a system are data input; validation/integration; analysis, synthesis, interpretation, and extrapolation; reporting to functional areas; decisions, action plans, and goals; and measurement of planned actions. Customer satisfaction measurement should be a closed loop of information, sensitive and self-adjusting. It should function like a thermostat controlling temperature in a building, or an autopilot flying an airplane. Find out what customers want, and give it to them.

## Who Is the Customer?

If you listen to the wrong "customer," what you hear may be irrelevant. Put too heavy a weight on attitudes among one sector of influencers while ignoring another, and the resulting decisions can be disastrously misguided. While it is not possible to accurately weigh the influence of all the people who affect your distribution chain, it is possible to apply customer satisfaction measurement techniques and technology to all of the links. Where discrepancies exist, common sense usually dictates whose opinions matter the most. There are many industries where there is schizophrenia about who the customer is. Identification is an important issue to resolve strategically. One customer who is too often slighted is the internal customer.

## Surveys

Organizations make mistakes and miscalculations every day in regard to surveys. In the customer satisfaction field, the consequences of amateurism can be serious. For many executives, an experiment in customer satisfaction measurements begins—and ends—with a home-grown survey. There is a lot more to it than that, but it is also important to understand that the survey subject alone is more complex than it might appear at first.

## Compensation

Should incentive compensation be tied to customer satisfaction measurement? The direct answer is yes, but the pathway to that end is strewn with rocks. It involves the whole issue of how employees are motivated. It also has to do with fairness. Critical issues must be dealt with: establishment of customer satisfaction as a basic value; a customer satisfaction measurement system that produces reliable results; awareness of the effect people have on customer satisfaction; clarity of management's long-term commitment; involving everyone in a collaborative process to devise systems acceptable as fair; and linkage of everyone's compensation, including executives, to customer satisfaction.

## Production/Operations

In the customer satisfaction field, little attention is paid to the people who actually make and deliver products: the factory workers, the machine operators, the assemblers, the warehouse workers. Management people who distance themselves from this area of the business are missing important opportunities for competitive advantage; at the same time, they are increasing the likelihood of quality problems and employee disaffection. There are several ways to involve workers in customer satisfaction: Communicate customer satisfaction measurement results; adopt Baldrige Award criteria; invite customers in to meet the workers; send workers out to meet the customers; involve workers with suppliers; and create an employee suggestion system that really works.

# *Part One*

# MANAGEMENT CONSIDERATIONS

The book is divided into four parts, each of which represents a cluster of ideas. Part One deals with high-level considerations that normally fall within the purview of top executives. While the decision making on these matters rests at the top of organizations, the impact is important for everyone. Like the tremors of an earthquake, they are felt everywhere.

Management has been described as the art of asking the right questions. Part One is intended to prompt readers, whether top executives or those affected by top-executive decision making, to ask questions about the ramifications of customer satisfaction. What role does the customer play in the vision of the organization? What is involved in creating a customer-centered culture? If you are serious about embracing customer satisfaction, how will it change the organization? How can you factor the customer into planning?

# 1
# Measurement Magic

There is magic in measurement.

Imagine that you are the newly appointed police commissioner for the City of New York. The city is riddled with crime, and it's getting worse every year. The conventional wisdom is that lawbreaking is caused by societal factors beyond law enforcement's control. So what can you hope to accomplish?

That was the picture when William J. Bratton became police commissioner in January 1994. Since then, major crime rates have been reduced from 15 to 20 percent a year, far better than other major cities and the nation as a whole. What happened?

One of the first things Bratton did was to define the task. The job of the NYPD, he said, is *to cut crime*, plainly and simply, regardless of societal factors. He then made clear that the *measure of success* would be a decrease in the crime rate.

When Bratton arrived on the job, crimes were being tracked with colored pins and wall maps. Citywide data were months old before they were assembled at headquarters. He insisted that crime data be computerized and collected *daily*. Precinct commanders were to face the data at weekly meetings. It was management by fact, in the extreme, a sharp contrast to fuzzy assumptions and rationalizations.

Bratton's approach to managing his huge department, with its thirty-five thousand uniformed cops, was straightforward. His seventy-six precinct commanders were left to manage their resources as they saw fit—provided crime continued to go down in their territory. If it didn't, the weekly meetings with their peers would get pretty uncomfortable.

To expose his top people to the way private-sector organizations think, Bratton invited corporate chieftains to so-called executive breakfasts. He subsequently left for a job in private industry. Actually there are many companies that could learn from Bratton's leadership of the New York police some things about clarity of purpose and the effectiveness of measurement.

A company clearly defining its purpose as *improving the satisfaction of its customers* would be analogous to New York cops knowing that their job is to cut crime. Installation of comprehensive customer satisfaction measurement methods, processes, and systems is analogous to replacing pins and wall maps with daily computerized tracking.

In many organizations the idea of customer satisfaction measurement doesn't get much beyond taking an annual customer satisfaction survey. Often the surveys are developed internally by persons untrained in opinion research. In such cases the results are rarely used to influence decision making at the top levels.

For an organization to become truly customer-centered, much more is needed than an occasional survey and a complaint-handling system. A comparison can be drawn with the quality movement. Companies learned they needed more than statistical process control to achieve quality; they needed to develop a quality culture from top to bottom. Customer-centered companies must develop a culture that allows the customer to be the driving force.

# Processes of the Customer-Centered Organization

The model for a customer-centered organization (Figure 1-1) includes these processes:

• *Data Input.* There are at least thirty different ways that organizations can monitor and measure what their customers think, feel, and do. The customer survey is only one way. No single source of customer information, or limited combination of sources, is adequate. Multiple sources are needed to develop a full understanding of what data mean. For example, it is important not only to know what customers say but to cross-check that against what they do.

Figure 1-1. The closed loop of customer satisfaction measurement.

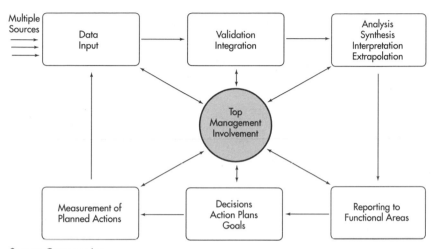

*Source:* Customer Inc.

In designing a customer satisfaction measurement (CSM) system, a good beginning is to identify the channels of CSM presently in existence (most organizations have several), track how the information flows and is used in the organization, and identify gaps and weaknesses.

• *Validation/Integration.* You may be tempted to react to fragments of information. Unvalidated information often is misleading and the cause of poor decisions. Impressions from surveys can be probed more deeply using focus groups. What people say they want can be cross-checked against sales data showing actual buying decisions. More often than not, single data points (snapshots) are relatively meaningless; you have to track trends. Since there are pluses and minuses to every research technique, it is important to integrate data from multiple sources to increase confidence in findings.

• *Analysis/Synthesis.* Many organizations complain of drowning in data, even while they say they're lacking information and knowledge. This occurs when inadequate attention is paid to analysis, synthesis, interpretation, and extrapolation. There are many statistical analysis techniques, Charting and graphing (see Figure 1-1) help bring clarity to data. Management can play an important role by insisting on analytical reports expressed clearly in plain English.

• *Reporting.* Existing channels of CSM data often are dead-ended. The data stop at the desk of a supervisor in customer service, shipping, finance, sales, or some other department. In some cases it is ignored, in others suppressed. In an effective CSM system, the results are reported to functional departments in language they can understand and in a form they can respond to. This is how information should emerge from the analysis/synthesis step in the process.

• *Decisions.* Everything up to this point is merely sound and fury unless it results in decisions, action plans, and goals. For this to occur, CSM must be an integral part of planning (both strategic and operational), budgeting, compensation, and incentive programming. CSM must be in the mainstream of decision making, not the ad hoc exercise it often is. When this occurs, organizations are firmly on the path to becoming customer-centered.

• *Measurement.* When plans are decided upon as a result of CSM, they have the virtue of being measurable using CSM methods. With any action taken to improve customer satisfaction, the results can be measured and performance against goals established. Although the ultimate measure shows up in financial performance, that is a lagging indicator. CSM, properly done, is more immediate and hence a more sensitive tool for use in management decision making.

As seen in Figure 1-1, the steps identified above constitute a closed loop that continues to cycle and repeat itself. In company after company you can see that this process occurs only if top management involves itself every step of the way, continuously. Top executives are tugged and pulled in so many different directions that it is not uncommon for them to resist taking direct responsibility for a function like CSM. This changes once they see CSM as integral to their ultimate responsibility for shaping corporate culture, strategic planning, and financial performance.

# The Malcolm Baldrige Award

An important step forward in the development of CSM occurred with the creation of the Malcolm Baldrige National Quality Award in 1987. It places heavy emphasis on customer satisfaction as the driver for quality. As the public law establishing the award stated, "Strategic planning for quality and quality improvement programs, through a commitment to excellence in manufacturing and services, are becoming more and more essential to the well-being of our Nation's economy and our ability to compete effectively in the global marketplace."

The award criteria were designed to help companies enhance their competitiveness through a focus on two results-oriented goals:

1. Delivery of ever-improving value to customers, resulting in marketplace success
2. Improvement of overall company performance and capabilities

From the outset, the designers of the Baldrige Award, prominent leaders from virtually every sector of American business, recognized that quality is determined by customers. In linking award criteria to key business issues, Baldrige Award criteria states: "Customer-driven quality places major emphasis on the 'positive side of quality,' which stresses enhancement, new services, and customer relationship management. Success with the positive side of quality depends heavily on creativity—usually more so than steps to reduce errors and defects, which tend to rely more on well-defined techniques."[1]

The Baldrige scoring system has a total possible score of 1,000. Winners usually score in the 600–700 range. Of the 1,000 possible points in Baldrige, 250 are in the category of Customer Focus and Satisfaction. Here is how the category is described:

> *Customer and Market Knowledge.* Describe how the company determines near-term and longer-term requirements and expectations of customers and markets, and develops listening and learning strategies to understand and anticipate needs.
>
> *Customer Relationship Management.* Describe how the company provides effective management of its responses and follow-ups with customers to preserve and build relationships and to increase knowledge about specific customers and about general customer expectations.
>
> *Customer Satisfaction Determination.* Describe how the company determines customer satisfaction, customer repurchase intentions, and customer satisfaction relative to competitors; describe how these determination processes are evaluated and improved.
>
> *Customer Satisfaction Results.* Summarize the company's customer satisfaction and customer dissatisfaction results using key measures and/or indicators of these results.
>
> *Customer Satisfaction Comparison.* Compare the company's customer satisfaction results with those of competitors.

# Customer Satisfaction Index

A number of companies have developed Customer Satisfaction Index (CSI) approaches that help divisions, departments, or other organizational entities keep score of their customer satisfaction performance. The ones that have been most successful carefully guard against using CSI data punitively against employees or managers.

Employees respond well to measurement when they have latitude and encouragement to improve their performance, and confidence that the measurements do not threaten their livelihood. Besides, people have a natural tendency to want to keep score.

# Diagnostic Tools

An index is a diagnostic tool. To use a medical analogy, doctors monitor vital signs, order X-rays, CAT scans and MRIs, and run other tests in order to diagnose the ailments of patients. There are many channels of information that can be used to understand relationships with customers.

The customer satisfaction measurement professional is a diagnostician, with numerous analytical tools available. They can be grouped as research methods, operational data, marketing/sales channels, and other. Here are examples:

### Research Methods

Customer surveys
Dealer/supplier surveys
Mystery shoppers
Customer visits (to you/to
   them)

Employee surveys
Focus groups
Customer panels
Industry trade press

### Operational Data

Complaints
Customer comment cards

Field service reports
Product returns
Telephone activity reports

Customer service reports
Engineering/design
   meetings
Warranty claims
Employee suggestions
Quality performance
   tracking

### Marketing/Sales Channels

| | |
|---|---|
| Sales contact reports | Customer/competitor advertising |
| Trade show intelligence | Sales data analysis |
| Lead tracking | Closed accounts |
| New product idea suggestions | Customer literature |

### Other

| | |
|---|---|
| Benchmarking | Management contacts |
| Workshops/seminars | Business literature |

Different couplings of data help provide a true picture of where you stand with your customers. For example, customer surveys and focus groups might show that one of the things your customers consider most important is for you to ship their orders complete. Operational data might show that only 75 percent of shipments go out complete as ordered. Thus 25 percent of the time you are failing to do something that is important to customers.

These data can then be compared to complaints and information on closed accounts to help calculate the impact on your business. Further research could let you know how you are doing in comparison to competitors on this one critical performance criterion. Benchmarking against companies that perform well on ship-to-order criteria could provide ideas for improving your performance.

Ultimately, bringing all of this information together helps management in making critical decisions on where to place priorities and where to allocate resources for technology, training, incentives, management expertise, etc. Finally, the same measurements that pinpoint areas needing attention can also be used to measure the effectiveness of remedies.

# Analytical Tools

Making sense out of the information garnered from diagnostic tools requires analysis. The analytical tools available for dealing with customer satisfaction measurement data are many and varied. Most are familiar to professionals in the quality field: flowcharts, brain-storming, nominal group technique, Delphi analysis, scatter plots, X-bar charts, six-sigma analysis, run charts, factor analysis, Pareto charts, histo-grams, cause-and-effect diagrams, and force field analysis.

Under most circumstances, it is not necessary for managers to learn advanced statistical methods. Use of such familiar techniques as means, proportions, weighting factors, and simple cross-tabulations is suffi-cient.

It is a bit more complicated in the beginning when CSM programs are being designed. At this stage, it is usually necessary to examine large numbers of variables simultaneously, which calls for some form of multivariate analysis, such as factor analysis, multiple regressions, or discriminant analysis.

On close examination, it becomes evident that customer satisfac-tion measurement involves comprehensive information systems and sophisticated analysis and reporting processes. Obviously, there is a great deal more to it than a few management utterances about satisfying or delighting customers and an annual "customer sat" survey—as use-ful and interesting as that might be.

An analogy can be drawn with the often misunderstood terms of marketing and sales. Everyone understands sales as what it takes to ring the cash register by persuading people to buy things. Marketing, on the other hand, involves databases, market segmentation, pricing, demographics, psychographics, advertising, promotion, packaging, distribution systems, etc. Marketing is highly analytical and disci-plined. Sales is more freewheeling relationship building.

Customer satisfaction measurement is analogous to marketing. Frontline customer service is analogous to sales.

## Internal Customer Satisfaction

Often overlooked or misunderstood in all of this is the importance of the internal customer, otherwise known as *employees*. It is impossible to satisfy the external customer for long if your own people are not fulfilled, rewarded, listened to, and happy in their work. Front-line employees won't remain enthusiastic without the support and encour-agement of their organization. Interdepartmental feuding and dissatis-faction saps organizational strength.

It is as important to measure internal customer satisfaction as it is external. Apart from the point of view of morale and corporate culture, employees have their fingers on the pulse of the customer to a far greater degree than management does. Employees are a source of knowledge, experience, and ideas of incalculable value.

The employee resource goes numb if people are not asked for their ideas and opinions and if their thoughts, when expressed, are ignored. With the focus on customers, and with employees viewed as internal customers, the culture of an organization changes in many positive ways.

Hollow talk and clichés about satisfying corporate customers are viewed cynically by employees, unless accompanied by the disciplines of CSM. Without the discipline, it's all sales talk, unsupported by the grunt work of marketing.

## The Truly Customer-Centered Company

Few would argue with Edward M. Marshall, a noted change management consultant who says the workplace of the twenty-first century "must be passionately focused on the customer. The members of the workforce must be aligned with and own the strategic direction of the business, have trust-based work relationships, and be able to build value with one another and their customers."[2]

What does it take to be a truly customer-centered company?

- Top management must be unwaveringly committed to having a company that is truly customer-driven, and they must reinforce the commitment forcefully and consistently.
- Whenever important decisions are to be made on any aspect of the business, the most important question is always "What is best for our customers?"
- A minimum of six channels of information must be employed to acquire customer satisfaction information; it is then displayed statistically and charted or graphed regularly to show trends.
- There must be processes, systems, and procedures in place for making decisions based on customer satisfaction measurement findings; the same goes for measuring the accomplishment and success of the actions taken.
- All employees must understand and be able to explain that their primary function and accountability is to serve customers, either internal or external.
- At least to some degree, compensation and incentives for all employees must be linked to customer satisfaction measurement.

# Why Change Initiatives Fail

Only a few standout companies can claim to meet all of these criteria. Many more will be able to do so in the future as CSM hits its stride. In the meantime, becoming customer-centered likely means significant change, a process that is proving difficult for many companies. Why is it so common for change initiatives to fail? Numerous studies on the reasons for failure can be summarized:

- *Half-heartedness.* Talk is insufficient without the understanding that keeps people from wavering and pulling back from the complexities and trauma of genuine change; wholehearted "stick-to-itiveness" is the only way to succeed.
- *Lack of shared vision.* Key members of a management team must agree on the vision and communicate it, both by action and words, consistently and for the long term, until the vision is fully absorbed into the corporate culture and psyche.
- *Failure to install reinforcing mechanisms.* To encourage buy-in, and to release creative energy and enthusiasm at all levels of the organization, it is essential to have processes, reward systems, and recognition linked to the goals of change.

There is a paradox at work here. Businesses tend to be internally focused, that is, preoccupied with organizational structure, systems and programs, while frankly admitting that the most important forces at work upon them are external. While busying themselves with technical administrivia, thoughtful executives acknowledge that their biggest problems are people-related or cultural.

# Where Does Customer Satisfaction Measurement Fit In?

The risk of failure in efforts to change is sharply reduced by choosing a strategy of becoming truly customer-centered. Why is this so?

- *Look at the record.* As this book shows, there is overwhelming evidence that companies working at becoming customer-centered make more money, grow faster, and have happier, more-fulfilled employees than those that aren't.

- *It's a strategy with staying power.* The customer is everchanging. Commitment to the customer is a job that's never done. Unlike such initiatives as product quality, reengineering, or profitability goals, customer satisfaction is less prone to being viewed as a program that can or will ever be "finished."
- *The virtue of simplicity.* Commitment to the customer is a vision that can be simply explained and easily understood at all levels of an organization, and one to which people can commit with conviction and enthusiasm.
- *It can be measured.* This form of management by fact is possible because there are many ways to measure customer satisfaction so that it can be incorporated into processes and systems that help people throughout the organization keep score and see the results of their efforts.

# References

1. 1995 Baldrige Award Criteria, p. 17.
2. E. M. Marshall,*Transforming the Way We Work* (New York: AMA-COM, 1995), p. 3.

# 2

# Vision

There are, no doubt, many reasons why George Bush lost his bid for reelection to the presidency in 1992. One of them certainly was that the public believed his critics, who said he lacked a vision for the country. It didn't help when Bush responded with a put-down about "the vision thing."

In business there is also a tendency to be flip about "the vision thing." It's a serious mistake. Leadership experts contend that an attractive, worthwhile, and achievable vision of the future, widely shared, is a driving force toward excellence and success.

## The Elements of Vision

The words I've just mentioned deserve thoughtful consideration by leaders striving to raise their sights above tree-top level.

### The Vision Is Attractive

The vision the leader presents to the organization must be alluring. It must have qualities that people gravitate toward because it represents a future that is more desirable than the present. The right vision is exciting enough to call forth the skills, talents, and resources to make it happen.

The founding fathers had such a vision when they wrote the Constitution of the United States and the Bill of Rights. Abraham Lincoln had such a vision when he held the Union together through the incomprehensible trauma of the Civil War.

To be attractive and sustain that appeal, a vision must seem to have the gasp-value of a big idea. Small dreams vaporize under the relentless onslaught of daily activity. To justify being termed a *vision*, an idea must extend beyond the trivial and commonplace.

## The Vision Is Worthwhile

The problem with many so-called visions is that they are selectively worthwhile. For example, increasing shareholder value may seem highly worthwhile for a handful of company officers who hold juicy stock options, but it is pretty ho-hum to workers who don't own any stock at all.

Visions centering on profitability pull the heartstrings of the select few employees who enjoy direct benefits. Virtually everyone knows a business must be profitable to continue in existence. But that's not an idea that catapults people out of bed in the morning. In the same way, a vision about downsizing and improving productivity doesn't turn on people who expect to be victims of the effort. And a self-serving vision of working toward winning corporate awards and recognition doesn't mean much to people who aren't going to attend the awards banquet.

## The Vision Is Achievable

Many vision statements suffer from pie in the sky, a lack of credibility. Back when big companies were duking it out in the mainframe computer business, the National Cash Register Company spent big bucks on an advertising campaign claiming that "NCR Means Computers." It was amusing to people who knew that NCR meant cash registers; IBM meant computers.

Those people knew a vision of NCR meaning computers was not achievable; far from energizing an entire organization, it was a frothy, empty statement. This is not to say that a vision shouldn't involve stretch goals; by definition a vision is a dream of what can be in the future. But it must at least seem possible to those asked to commit their lives to it.

## The Vision Is Widely Shared

The term *shared vision* appears often in current business writings. There are two elements to this concept: shared and vision. First, the vision must be *worthy* of being shared, that is, attractive, worthwhile, and achievable. Without these qualities, a vision simply lacks relevance for most people.

## Communicating Your Vision

Beyond clarifying the nature of the vision lies the difficult task of communicating it and gaining acceptance. It takes time and persistence for even the most compelling of visions to be fully absorbed into an organization. To move from awareness to understanding to acceptance to commitment can be agonizingly slow; it occurs at different rates for different people.

If the vision has been well articulated and has the involvement and support of most people, the organization is said to be in alignment.

For a vision of being truly customer-centered to be viable, the leader formulating the vision must understand fully what it means to the organization. It has no power if it is only a slogan lacking the support necessary for significant change.

It is common, in fact, for pronouncements about customer satisfaction to be chimerical, with management never intending to undertake the cultural change necessary to make words into reality. Either managers don't understand the kind of sweeping change that is needed, or they are engaging in wishful thinking that saying will make it so without much effort or expense.

When the thought of building a vision around the idea of being customer centered first gets considered, there is a risk it will be discounted as a banal oversimplification. Any organization could have that as a vision, couldn't it? Certainly something more is needed than a one-size-fits-all generality akin to motherhood and the flag.

## Developing Your Vision

Every organization is distinct when it comes to fleshing out what customer satisfaction really means in its environment. The simple concept of devoting the enterprise to satisfying customers is like the first sketch in a storyboard intended ultimately to become a virtual-reality computer program.

A fully developed customer satisfaction vision for a retail business might extend to exotic ways of building databases that capture the uniqueness of each customer, making possible one-to-one marketing techniques refined to a degree barely imaginable now.

For a university, the vision might be to revolutionize learning by developing individually tailored programs of study for each student, utilizing the latest in information technology, and providing a version of such university services to businesspeople pursuing the current interest in concepts of the "learning organization."

For a precision machining company, the vision might be to develop communication processes with customers that would allow them to integrate operations so that designing, ordering, and scheduling happen as though the two companies were one, eliminating the traditional sales and purchasing functions and the costs associated with them, a wholly new way of doing business.

At the heart of each of these vision ideas is the concept of responding to customer wants, needs, and desires. The thinking, visualizing, and dreaming starts where it should—with the customer—and then grows into a full-blown vision around which an organization can be built. This is quite different from visioning exercises that begin with a review of available resources (human and material), market share, product life cycles, discretionary capital, competition, and economic prognostications. Visions that arise from this kind of thinking tend to be predictable and unimaginative.

Although arriving at the right vision for an organization can be arduous and may come not through logic but in a flash of inspiration, there are disciplines that can be applied to help determine whether the vision is right.

Ideas can be narrowed down to a reasonable set of alternative visions and then ordered according to which seem most promising. Starting at the top of the list, test the vision alternatives (1) against the desired properties of a good vision; (2) for consistency with your organization's culture, values, strengths, and stakeholders; and (3) with scenarios of your organization's future external environment.

Finally, the vision must be stated as clearly as possible. Then check it out with trusted colleagues. See whether your words mean the same thing to them as they do to you. If the message is not easily understood and readily accepted, you need to modify either the vision or how it is expressed.

## Live the Vision

Anything as important as a vision intended to chart the future course of an organization must be communicated effectively, using all available communications resources. And of course, this needs to be done with diligence and persistence over an extended period of time. There is, however, a critical factor that is not obvious and is often slighted: The CEO has to get out in front and live the vision. The CEO's most important obligation is to bring life to a vision through demonstration and performance. Failure to do so is picked up instantaneously by the organization. If the organizational reality is that people are expected to do what the CEO says but not what he or she does, the cause is lost.

Leaders must take the first step because doing so demonstrates their faith in the idea, program, or service. Going first demonstrates the leader's commitment.

When Corning adopted a vision of achieving world-class quality, CEO James R. Houghton reportedly devoted a quarter of his time on quality-related activities. He visited more than forty Corning locations around the world each year to emphasize the quality message. Corning's senior vice president and corporate director of quality, David B. Luther, became president and subsequently chairman of the American Society for Quality Control, very demanding work that showed clearly how committed he and his company were to quality.

While his boss was visiting Corning facilities, Luther spent a lot of time visiting customers to find out how Corning could serve them better. He recalls talking to a worker in a warehouse, asking him for his impressions about the Corning products they handled. "Since you asked," the worker said, "the only problem is the print on the labels on the boxes is so small we can't read it when the boxes are stacked at the top of the shelves." Luther assured him it was a problem easily fixed. A small matter, perhaps, but it affected efficiency in a customer's warehouse and the attitude of the customer's employees toward Corning. "It is a constant source of amazement to me," says Luther, "that companies make as little effort as they do to listen to their customers."[1]

By their actions, both Houghton and Luther breathed life into the company's vision, sending a powerful message to the employees of Corning that they were serious about quality and about the importance of customers in getting the big picture of quality.

## Ownership

It is also important to recognize that for a vision to matter—for it to instill energy into the daily lives of everyone in the organization—people need ownership of the vision and some idea of how they can help implement it through personal action.

This does not mean vision anarchy. Rather, the broad but appealing generalities of the typical vision statement have to translate to guidelines for behavior at the operating levels of the organization.

During World War II, the country's vision was clear to one and all: win the war by forcing the enemy's unconditional surrender. For individual soldiers, sailors, flyers, and marines, the vision called for courage, bravery, skill, conditioning, determination, and perseverance under the most horrendous conditions.

Experts on the subject of learning organizations stress the need for a shared vision. When the vision is not shared, lots of bad things occur. One problem is an obsession with consensus. At the root of a wishy-washy inability to take action, there is often belief that it is best to get agreement from everyone concerned. It *is* important to let everyone express themselves, but the goal should not be consensus.

This point is sometimes misunderstood by, for example, observers of the Japanese style of management. When a Japanese company undertakes a major new project, meetings are held—sometimes for days on end—to give everyone a chance to express themselves on how the project will affect them. By the time the project starts, everyone has had their say and all of the questions on people's minds have been asked and answered. From day one of the new project, everyone is working together.

Contrast that with the American management style. Typically, the order goes out from on high and is filtered down through the ranks of the hierarchy. Usually the message is garbled along the way. Inevitably glitches occur and reports on them go back up the chain of command, again getting garbled along the way. Directions on how to correct the glitches follow the same tortuous path. Huge amounts of energy are dissipated along the way.

Contrary to the impression some people have, the Japanese are not looking for consensus. Their goals are communication, understanding, and respect for workers at all levels of the organization. The American style—at least the classic one—seems based on some notion of Teutonic efficiency. As that has broken down, it has been replaced by a fuzzy retreat into consensus.

Consultants on learning organizations Peter Kline and Bernard Saunders explain the failure of consensus this way: "Consensus often leads to an appallingly mediocre state of affairs in which the collective IQ of the group is likely to be lower than that of the individual with the lowest IQ in the group. That's because conflicts tend to be resolved downward. If someone has an idea and anyone else objects, it is dropped. Therefore, the only ideas likely to be seriously considered are those acceptable to everyone, and these ideas are usually commonplace, unchallenging, and in many cases already widely accepted anyway. This tendency for groups to function at the level of their lowest common denominator leads to groupthink."[2]

A simple way to avoid the constipation of groupthink is to make customer satisfaction, not consensus, the recognized and accepted standard. The most penetrating question to ask at every meeting is, "What's best for our customers?" The tenor of the meeting is a lot different than when the question is, "What can we agree on?"

## Energize Your Organization

There are three basic things top management must do if it wishes to employ the power of vision to energize the organization:

- Formulate and communicate a vision that is attractive, achievable, worthwhile, and widely shared.
- Be out front for all to see in living the vision.
- Encourage a culture in which everyone is able to define their own share of the vision, their own piece of the rock.

## References

1. David Luther, personal communication.
2. Peter Kline and Bernard Saunders, *Ten Steps to a Learning Organization* (Arlington, Va.: Great Ocean Publishers, 1993).

# 3

# Culture

There is a breed of corporate executives out to prove their toughness by emphasizing a single-minded corporate objective: Shareholders come first. They obviously believe this kind of muscle-flexing is much admired and rewarded on Wall Street and in the boardroom. And often it is.

When Albert J. Dunlap became CEO of Scott Paper in 1994, he made this statement: "Shareholders are the number one constituency. Show me an annual report that lists six or seven constituencies, and I'll show you a mismanaged company."[1]

Dunlap's attitude flies in the face of common sense. There is also ample evidence that corporations do best for shareholders when they put all three constituencies—shareholders, customers, and employees—on the same plane. A savvy investor might say, "Show me an executive who makes a statement like that and I'm selling my stock."

## Shareholders *Don't* Come First

In the triumvirate of constituencies, customers are the primary activists when they decide whether or not to spend their money with the company. Next most crucial are the employees, whose work significantly influences the buying decisions of customers. The most passive—and arguably least interested—constituency is the stockholder, waiting and watching to react to how well the others do.

Whether he realized it or not, and he probably did, with his dogmatic statement Dunlap set the tone for the corporate culture of Scott

Paper. By contrast, *Fortune* magazine wrote in announcing its 1995 selection of America's Most Admired Corporations: "If there is one characteristic that sets the top-ranking companies of the Most Admired apart, it is their robust cultures. The culture of a company, a good proxy for character in a person, drives reputation. And like character, culture guides and defines its host body, allowing it to anticipate change and grow while remaining true to some core self."[2]

Nobody seriously discounts the importance of shareholder value in the total mix of business. But to stress it to the exclusion of other considerations is an insult to employees and customers—who are not, by the way, unaware of such things. Employees know the CEO is likely to make a ton of money as a sycophant to stockholders. They can be forgiven their cynicism. Customers rightfully take umbrage at any hint that they don't come first with the companies they buy from.

# Financial Analysts Would Boggle

Dunlap stepped to the helm at Scott Paper at a time when sales had gone flat. He hiked prices, sold assets, cut costs, and eliminated more than eleven thousand jobs. His message to everyone in the company, repeated over and over, was "not to spend a dime unless it added to shareholder value."

That's asking a lot of people who couldn't have even the vaguest idea of how to weigh their decisions against the ultimate effect on shareholder value. It is a challenge that would boggle even the most sophisticated financial analyst armed with full data and a monster computer. The chain of activity that determines stockholder value defies analysis.

Could it be that Dunlap's goal all along was what then happened in July 1995? Scott Paper was acquired by Kimberly-Clark in a $6.8 billion deal. Dunlap was retained as an advisor to the Kimberly-Clark board; apparently they admired the way he had restructured Scott. It will be interesting to see whether the newly combined companies follow Dunlap's orthodoxy or instead heed a more enlightened approach of putting all three major stakeholder groups equally at the forefront.

Many of the most admired companies in fact do exactly the opposite of what Dunlap proclaimed. In their annual reports, Motorola, Harris Corp., Eastman Chemical, and others do talk about the equal importance of all stakeholders.

Unfortunately, many of the most admired group also admit that they aren't systematically analyzing relations with these key constituencies. And it gets worse when you explore the compensation aspect of the equation: failing to pay people according to how well they do in serving customers, internal and external. It is relatively rare to find customer satisfaction metrics and indices of employee satisfaction embedded in executive compensation plans.

It's reasonable to conclude that the basis for corporate culture is only slowly coming to a balanced view of the role of the corporation in society. Financial trade publications do note that chief financial officers are beginning to pay attention to balance in the delivery of shareholder value with the delivery of value to other stakeholders.

The issue, plain and simple, is one of corporate culture. Says *Fortune*, "Yes, culture, that sometimes fuzzy concept first fashionable years ago, is now raising its head again, even after years of financially focused restructuring." The article goes on, almost poetically: "As a company navigates this roiling sea of change without the old buoys of hierarchy and supervision, the constellations of beliefs and values that make up its culture reemerge as the stars to steer by. The knowledge worker, you may by now have tired of hearing, is more self-directed than the industrial worker; his work is more a matter of deciding what to do and how to do it than of doing what he's told. Culture provides the context for such decisions. . . . Values are a healthy substitute for the kind of stultifying systems that make big organizations unwieldy, unresponsive—and unadmired."[3]

So what values should be stressed? Shareholder value? Honesty? Integrity? Concern for the interests of employees? The primacy of the customer? Hard work? Creativity? Making the numbers? Growth? Profits? Reputation? Quality? Boldness? Appearance? Character?

# No Customer, No Money

There is logic to putting the customer first. Criminal investigators talk of following the money trail. Well, the money trail starts with the customer. No customer, no money; no money, no company. Anyone and everyone can understand that. What is not so easily understood is how everything else falls into line once customers are granted their rightful place.

The shareholder-first concept has already been discussed. There are some companies that advocate putting employees first, on the theory that only employees who are treated right can and will do a good job for customers. True, but the sequence is a bit wobbly, because it is possible for contented employees to fail in their responsibilities to customers. But with the customer-first imperative, it takes satisfied employees to achieve that objective. It then becomes clear that the organization must pay attention to all of the elements that go into creating and sustaining good morale—which is obviously a key ingredient in the primary objective of putting the customer first.

When customer satisfaction and employee satisfaction are healthy and vigorous, a solid and loyal customer base is established. Although it doesn't show up on a balance sheet, this is the greatest asset any company can have. It is this asset that results in sales, and in turn profits, and finally shareholder value.

Other stakeholders are, of course, important: suppliers, distributors, the community, government, even the industry of which the company is a part. All are dependent, to one degree or another, on the company's surviving and succeeding. In other words, all are dependent on that very first action: a customer making a purchase.

The logic is so simple—so clear, solid, indisputable—that it is amazing in how many ways companies can do violence to it.

## Every Corporation Has a Culture

Corporate culture is complex, but one thing about it is clear. It isn't something you can have or not have. There is a way of thinking about things and a way of doing things in every organization; that is what constitutes its culture. Employees may not be able to articulate it, but they know what it is and it governs their actions day to day.

Among companies steeped in tradition, there are cultural folkways so strong as to be ironclad rules of behavior. In others, the influence of culture is subtler and harder to pinpoint. Some executives have a strong, intuitive grasp of the culture in their organization and are adept at shaping it. Other executives are so out of touch that they don't even sense the cultural mores around them. CEOs who think about their influence on corporate culture may find it helpful to ask themselves three questions periodically:

1. What are my responsibilities, in order of priority?
2. What percentage of my time is spent reinforcing a culture based on our corporate values?
3. Do my actions and priorities demonstrate a commitment to customer satisfaction?

# GE: A Model for Effective Cultural Change

One company that has done an extraordinary job of changing its culture is General Electric. To start the process, CEO Jack Welch shocked the complacent and entrenched executive bureaucrats at GE by telling them in no uncertain terms that there was going to be a revolution in the company.

In his book on the GE transformation, Noel Tichy writes, "the ultimate goal of the revolution is for all employees to act for the good of the company without having to wait for orders. That means getting people to face facts and take responsibility—an astoundingly difficult thing to achieve, especially in large organizations."

It has taken over a decade for Welch to achieve his objectives, and he has done it by constantly repeating and reinforcing clear statements of values. Here is a statement of some of the values that were debated and adopted by GE's management corps:

- Only satisfied customers can provide job security.
- Change is continual, thus nothing is sacred. Change is accepted as the rule rather than the exception.
- Leaders share knowledge rather than withholding it as an element of power. Everyone benefits when they know what the leader knows—nothing is "secret."
- Paradox is a way of life. You must function collectively as one company and individually as many businesses at the same time. For us, leadership means leading while being led, producing more output with less input.
- We encourage the sharing of these values because we believe they are both fair and effective, but we realize they are not for everyone.... Individuals whose values do not coincide with these expressed preferences will more likely flourish better outside the General Electric Company.[4]

The intellectual home for the transformation at GE was the company's management training center in Croton-on-Hudson, New York. Every manager spends time there, taking courses of one kind and another. Welch is there a great deal, listening, debating, and arguing with managers from all levels of the company. It is the fount of the company's value system.

# Cultural Development Is the CEO's Job

At Home Depot, number five on *Fortune's* list of America's most admired corporations, founders Bernard Marcus, CEO, and Arthur Blank, president, continue to lead training sessions even though the company now has seventy thousand employees. The magazine cites Marcus as saying, "Nobody else does training this way. It's time-consuming, it's hard work." Obviously these wealthy and successful executives see development of corporate culture as an important part of their job. Comments *Fortune*, "The CEO as chief training officer? Get used to it. How else do you instill the right culture in a company?"[5]

# References

1. Bill Birchard, "How Many Masters Can You Serve?" *CFO Magazine* (July 1995), p. 49.
2. Rahul Jacob, "Corporate Reputations," *Fortune* (March 6, 1995), p. 56.
3. Ibid., p. 60.
4. Noel M. Tichy and Stratford Sherman, *Control Your Destiny or Someone Else Will* (New York: Doubleday, 1993), p. 143.
5. Jacob, "Corporate Reputations," p. 60.

# 4

# Change

Lawrence A. Bossidy, the CEO of Allied Signal, made this profound statement: "As we get more and more customer focused, we don't need to preach the need to change. People know it."[1]

The management of every organization is facing a perplexing question: How do you get people to participate willingly in something they don't like (change) if the survival of the organization depends on it?

## Fear of the Unknown

For those who view life in black-and-white terms, the answer seems simple. Just explain that change is necessary and everyone will go along. But why are human beings so resistant to change even when their present circumstances are less-than-ideal? Often it is fear of change: The devil you know is better than the devil you don't.

There is a word for the fear or hatred of change: misoneism. It is deeply ingrained in the human psyche. When its power is unrecognized by leaders trying to transform organizations, the best of intentions are doomed. Usually the defeat of change initiatives occurs in subtle, insidious ways that are endlessly frustrating to leaders.

Rarely do people dig in their heels and stubbornly refuse to change. More typically they overtly acknowledge that change is necessary and display enthusiasm for the idea of change. They may say, "It's about time. I've known for ages that things need to change around here." Then the sabotage begins—quietly, almost imperceptibly.

It is not so much that people fear change; after all, it can be exciting and invigorating. They fear uncertainty, the handmaiden of change. When the outcome of change initiatives that could affect them is uncertain, they employ a variety of tactics, conscious and subconscious, to slow things down.

Benign neglect is a time-honored technique: "Let's not deal with that right now; there are more important things to be done." Another approach is to avoid making decisions: "Let's buck it up the line." "Let's form a committee to study it." "There's no budget." "We don't have the authority." "It's not our job."

Organizations can be frozen in place when inaction and decision avoidance become ingrained in the culture. People who behave in this fashion are not malicious or incompetent, nor are they small-minded and driven by self-destructive impulses. They are just human beings, exhibiting misoneism.

Many people, even those sensitive to the uncertainty of their work lives and its causes, tend to separate the notion of change from their day-to-day work. However, change is not something to deal with during a lull in real work. Change is an integral part of people's real work, no matter how difficult and uncomfortable an undertaking it may be.

## Self-Motivation Is the Key to Change

When you begin messing around with change, you tamper with the core assumptions on which people base their lives. Each person has a very personal, unique view of employer, job, and place in the world. He or she has a sense of self-worth, position in the organization, potential for growth and advancement, security or lack of it, relationships with peers and bosses, and, finally, some perception of the qualities and values of the organization. People cling to these things for their identity, right along with family, faith, nation, community, and tradition.

It is arrogance and folly for leaders of organizations to think they can change these ingrained belief patterns in an entire workforce by making a few speeches about the need for change and writing an occasional article in company publications. A column in the monthly "Bugle" cannot make people see things differently and behave accordingly.

Some executives think it is their responsibility, indeed their obligation, to advise people how they should think. That notion is part and parcel of the now-discredited concept of the hierarchical organization.

The attitude of "I'll do the bossing, you do the working" gets in the way of change.

There are still many people "running" organizations, in the misguided belief that you can motivate employees. You cannot. At best, motivational incentives can stimulate a short-term burst of activity. But even the most lavish award systems lose their impact rather quickly. The bonus is an example of an incentive that soon is viewed as an entitlement.

On the other hand, people also become inured to punishment. In carrot-and-stick motivational theory, the half-life of the stick is equally short. Its effectiveness wears off, usually rather quickly. Budget cuts and elimination of perks are soon taken for granted, failing to produce much in the way of behavior change.

Of course, there are organizations whose people are motivated. On close examination, we find that these organizations foster the only kind of motivation that really works long term: *self-motivation*. People perform with vigor and enthusiasm because they want to, not because they are being exhorted to.

## People Change Because They Want To

People make positive, progressive changes in the organizations they work for because they want to, not because they are being preached at incessantly. The issue then becomes, "What can we do that will make them want to change—want to badly enough to risk upsetting the apple cart of the status quo?"

To understand why people are reluctant to leave their organizational comfort zones—even when conditions are appalling—you need look no further than the kind of goals that traditional management is always talking about. "Profits. We need to improve our profits." "Shareholder value, that's what matters." "We need to right-size, get rid of the fat." "Our productivity needs to improve." "If we don't get more market share, we're in trouble." More new products, less bureaucracy, cost-cutting, efficiency, reduced waste, improved quality—blah, blah, blah. It is enough to weary even the most stalwart corporate servant. Notice the common denominator in all of these corporate directives. They are all internally focused. They are things "we" must do. Why? You can almost (but not quite) hear people muttering to themselves, "so management can make more money . . . have the next management meeting in Hawaii . . . buy another jet." Management people usually aren't that self-absorbed, self-serving and crass, but they risk coming across that way in organizations that lack a shared vision and purpose. Organizations are best able to adapt and change when there is alignment at all levels toward goals that make sense to everyone involved.

"In the years ahead, even a well-tuned business engine won't be enough. The winning corporations will be those that can create *human* engines, powered by turned-on, committed, responsible employees. Companies with old-fashioned, control-based organizations will disappear in the dust," writes Noel Tichy in *Control Your Destiny or Someone Else Will*, his book about the astonishing transformation that has occurred at GE. Tichy calls his book a handbook for revolutionaries. "The ultimate goal of the revolution," he says, , "is for all employees to act for the good of the company without having to wait for orders. That means getting people to face facts and take responsibility—an astoundingly difficult thing to achieve, especially in large organizations."[2]

## The Magnificent Obsession

There is a clear-cut, simple way to create an environment that fosters "turned-on, committed, responsible employees." Many companies flirt with it, but few have gone for it all the way, without timid reservations. It is one of those ideas that don't work very well if you make less than a 100 percent effort.

The idea is to get everyone in the organization focused on serving internal and external customers. When the organizational culture finds that that has become a kind of magnificent obsession, internal blockages to change dissipate. It is the shift in point of view that makes the difference. A note of caution: the shift has to be real. Lip service about delighting customers turns to corrosive cynicism when management makes decisions that are obviously anticustomer. When everyone knows that "delighting customers" is merely a hollow slogan, it has no power to inspire or influence.

It is interesting how Jack Welch "flirts" with customer satisfaction in some of the things he says. "The three most important things you need to measure in business," he asserts, "are customer satisfaction, employee satisfaction, and cash flow." Virtually in the same breath, however, he talks about the need for an overarching message, something big but simple and understandable, and gives examples: "We're going to be number one, or number two." "Fix / close / sell." Or "Boundarylessness." Note these are ideas with a predominantly internal focus, despite his previous expressions of concern about customer satisfaction. His mention of customer satisfaction measurement is lukewarm.

Meanwhile, Welch makes a good point that can be applied by organizations choosing to focus on customer satisfaction. Here's how Tichy quotes him: "Every organization needs values, but a lean organization needs them even more. When you strip away the support systems of staff and layers, people have to change their habits and expectations, or else the stress will just overwhelm them. We're all working harder and faster. But unless we're also having more fun, the transformation doesn't work. Values are what enable people to guide themselves through that kind of change."[3]

It is surprising that the message Welch keeps repeating is not that of customer satisfaction, which would be far more compelling and lasting than "We're going to be number one" and the others. The reason is that customer satisfaction represents a value that affects everyone, at all levels, every day. How often does the average worker make decisions that influence being number one or two? How often does a worker decide whether to fix, close, or sell an operation? How often does he or she consciously cross organizational boundaries?

But average employees do deal with customers—internal, external, or both—every day. Their performance *does* affect customers directly, influencing customer feelings about the organization. They *are* in a position to respond to problems and come up with ideas about how customer relationships can be improved. They *do* get ideas for new products and services as a result of customer contact.

When all the employees of an organization focus on customer satisfaction because *they want to,* as Bossidy said, "we don't need to preach the need to change. People know it." And something else very healthy also happens. Employees who are focused on customer satisfaction do not dissipate their energy in turf battles, company politics, griping, criticizing management, updating their resumes, protecting their perks, disagreeing with policy, sabotaging change, pursuing excessive self-interest, harboring dissatisfaction with pay and benefits, and the other negative acts that eat away at company morale.

## Establish Buy-In

One step is essential before an organization can adopt customer satisfaction as a guiding principle for change, although it is the toughest step of all. It is absolutely necessary to get buy-in, first from the key players and eventually from the entire workforce. Buy-in cannot be achieved by edict or force, or even good example. It has to be arrived at as a result of information and the opportunity to consider it.

The business literature is insisting, as if in a single voice, that business must change its ways or face dire consequences. Actually, it is pretty darn comfortable in the executive suite. There is a lot to be said for the world of multimillion-dollar executive paychecks, corporate jets, and the hushed splendor of offices befitting royalty. Why would people at the pinnacle of corporate success risk undermining their position by changing the rules of the game that got them there? The revolutionary hordes may be clamoring in the streets, but they can be pacified without changing the system. The solution in the minds of many executives is to talk about all the new concepts—but don't stray too far from the status quo.

# It Is Dangerous to Ignore the "Total" in Total Quality Management

Talk-but-don't-act is happening in businesses that confine quality activity to a Quality Department. Government departments, too, ignore the word *total* in total quality management as they talk reengineering but continue to be ruled by unthinking bureaucrats. The same is happening in organizations that think customer satisfaction consists of training service personnel to be more pleasant.

Either consciously or subconsciously, many people heading organizations are proceeding with organizational transformation, quality, customer satisfaction, reengineering, and other such initiatives in a manner that can only be described as half-hearted. They face a big problem: half-hearted won't work.

Organizations in today's fast-changing world can be compared to a huge building about to be cleared for urban renewal. The building looks solid. It has stood in all of its granite solidity for generations. Then, small but strategically placed charges of dynamite are detonated. Tiny puffs of white smoke appear, and the building collapses upon itself, destroyed in an instant by its own weight.

There are quite a number of small satchels that have the potential to implode large, stolid organizations today:

- Aggressive, turn-on-a-dime competitors
- International economics

- Galloping technology
- Product and service innovation
- Rot-from-within employee disaffection
- Acquisitions and mergers
- Uprisings by directors and stockholders
- Product obsolescence
- Disappearing markets

Like it or not, we live in a time of epochal change. As distasteful and unsettling as it may be, this is a time when leaders must diverge from comfortable traditions. It is a time when equivocating, as common as that resort is, is the worst choice.

For many executives, being in business is like being on an airplane in trouble. The engine is sputtering. You're standing in the doorway, parachute on your back, hesitating. Are you going to stand there, as many do, frozen by indecision? Or are you going to jump, trusting the parachute? In this little analogy, the parachute is a corporate culture that puts the customer first. In many companies, being truly customer-centered is about as different from their traditional ways of doing business as hanging from a parachute is compared to riding in a plane.

Jumping out of an airplane clarifies the meaning of commitment. There's no turning back. There's no "Oops, let's rethink this." That same level of commitment is required to achieve success with a customer satisfaction strategy. Unfortunately, when many executives say "customer service" it is a slip of the tongue.

An example of what happens when an organization decides to face the need for change head-on occurred at Chase Manhattan Bank. Twenty-four executives were subjected to a three-and-a-half-day soul-searching and strategic planning session at a conference center. A Chase executive commented: "The three and a half days is really a process of a series of breakdowns, early in the game, that force you to look at yourself and your peers, and your ideas about where you want to take the company. It leads to some pretty nasty behavior. Sometimes it pits people against one another. There were a number of arguments, and by the end of the first day we were, by design, in a place that was not very comfortable. People went to bed that night with twenty-four different views of the world, as well as a lot of anxiety about whether we might make things better or worse through this process."[4]

This kind of catharsis is often necessary before a clear vision is defined that everyone can commit to. A wise and sensitive facilitator is needed to guide independent-thinking executives through such a process.

Once the leadership group has settled on language describing a vision and a guiding principle comes the second step, equally challenging if not more so. The daunting task then is to obtain buy-in at all levels of the organization. Not just acquiescence or tolerance, but buy-in. This means everyone needs the opportunity to think about the vision and arrive at their own conclusions.

Just as at the executive level at the conference center, in obtaining organizationwide buy-in there are going to be arguments and disagreements. There may even be emotional outbursts and tears. So be it. Often there is no real progress in meetings until late at night when the pizza is cold and the soda pop has gone flat.

## Lack of Trust Is an Issue

A genuine, honest discussion that penetrates the surface of polite superficiality can occur only in an atmosphere of trust. But trust is sorely lacking in most organizations. As Mary Regnier, a consultant working in the field of organizational transformation, says, "when people open up you find out they don't trust their employers and co-workers. They fear being hurt by them."[5] Regnier likens these let-it-all-hang-out meetings to shattering glass: startling, frightening, unsettling. Her advice is to let the shattered glass lie there; don't try to clean it up quickly and pretend it never happened.

When people are asked to think about the vision for their organization, it is important that the discussion be led, not dictated; that it be conducted in an atmosphere of providing information instead of preapproved propaganda from on high. When this process is underway, it is difficult for many hard-driving, self-confident executives to be patient and listen. But if they are after meaningful change, then they must. Regnier puts it this way: "I sit and listen to executives tell me about their problems, how things are not working. Then they defend the way they are running things. I just look at them and say, 'I thought you just told me things aren't working. Are you ready to change or not?' "[6]

More than forty years ago, psychotherapist Carl R. Rogers wrote a classic article for the *Harvard Business Review* citing a communications issue that is as prevalent today as it was then. He wrote that "the major barrier to mutual interpersonal communication is our very natural tendency to judge, to evaluate, to approve (or disapprove) the statement of the other person or the other group." Rogers offered an example.

Commenting on a discussion, someone makes this statement: "I didn't like what the man said." How do you respond? Almost invariably, your reply is either approval or disapproval of the attitude expressed. You say, "I didn't, either; I thought it was terrible," or you reply, "Oh, I thought it was really good." In other words, your primary reaction is to evaluate it from *your* point of view, your own frame of reference.

Rogers offers a way to avoid this barrier to really listening and not judging. Here is how he put it: "Real communication occurs, and this evaluative tendency is avoided, when we listen with understanding. What does that mean? It means to see the expressed idea and attitude from the other person's point of view, to sense how it feels to him, to achieve his frame of reference in regard to the thing he is talking about. It is the most effective agent we know for altering the basic personality structure of an individual and for improving his relationships and his communications with others."[7]

# Self-Evaluation of the Leader

Every leader needs to examine his or her core beliefs about change. These are some of the questions to ask yourself:

- Am I willing to change myself, or do I really want to keep things as they are for myself while I implore others to change?
- Do I really understand that change doesn't mean the same thing now as it did earlier in my career?
- Have I accepted, at the core of my being, the reality that my business must change and change fast or else perish and perish fast?
- Have I been lulled into complacency by the idea that once you've done the TQM, delayering, reengineering, and empowering, it's okay to sit back and relax?

If you're like many executives, you'll say, "We're doing just fine . . . why change what's working?" Listen for a moment to the clarion call of two eminent seers.

Influential economist Paul Romer says managers had better brace themselves; the pace of economic change will only step up. The world of the hypereconomy, he says, is being driven by advances in technology that are every bit as influential as the traditional economic factors of capital and labor, if not more so.[8]

Tom Peters has a gift for cutting through gobbledygook and telling it like it is: "Believe Bob Dylan when he says the times they are a-changin'. And a-changin' damn near everything."

# References

1. Noel M. Tichy and Ram Charan, "An Interview With Lawrence A. Bossidy," *Harvard Business Review* (March-April 1995), p. 78.
2. Noel M. Tichy and Stafford Sherman, *Control Your Destiny or Someone Else Will* (New York: Doubleday, 1993).
3. Ibid.
4. Margery Stein, "Vision," *Corporate Meetings and Incentives* (June 1995), p. 26.
5. Interview with author.
6. Ibid.
7. Carl Rogers, "Barriers and Gateways to Communication," *Harvard Business Review* (July-August 1952).
8. Peter Robinson, "Paul Romer," *ASAP* (June 5, 1995), p. 67.

# 5

# Organization

In contemplating the idea of recognizing the customer as CEO, organization leaders should also ponder the Biblical admonition to not "putteth new wine into old bottles, else the new wine doth burst the bottles, and the wine is spilled, and the bottles will be marred." (Matthew 9:17)

Just as assuredly, the new wine of customer satisfaction will burst the old bottle of the rigid, top-down organization. Customer satisfaction will spill out on the ground, dissipating its potential. The organization will be marred by the disaffection of employees and the disappointment of customers.

Heads of organizations often are not ready for new bottles. Why should they be? They rose to the top through a system they have come to understand. It worked for them. It gave them power, wealth, recognition, prestige, respect. The organizations they head generally have momentum that is hard to stop.

Introducing customer satisfaction as the true driving force of an organization can be accomplished only when the shock waves to the organization are anticipated and welcomed. There is an interesting parallel with the organizational affliction known as "techno-narcissism": indulgence in high-tech pseudosolutions that don't work out in the marketplace. An example is the networking of information systems known as groupware, which eliminates the physical constraints of time, distance, and space. It is one of the most powerful collaborative technologies ever developed, so much so that IBM paid $3.5 billion for Lotus Development because its Notes software is a leader in groupware.

However, observers have pointed out that the potential of groupware is realized only if an organization is structured to take advantage of group work. Here is how *Business Week* characterized the situation editorially:

> Drop Notes into a company with a culture of individual competition and it's a waste of time and money. "Me-now" hotshots and "take charge" bosses are anathema to its success. If groupware is inserted into a flat, horizontal organization, it can boost productivity sharply. To make this new technology work, organization and culture are as important as PCS and software.
>
> Preaching collaboration is not enough. It is as important for companies to create incentives for people to share as it is for them to buy the latest groupware. Building cross-functional teams can work wonders in developing new products, but only if people are rewarded as members of the team. Right now, most individuals are still evaluated by their functional manager. That's one major reason why most teams fail to produce.
>
> In the end, groupware is a technology for managing relationships, not just information.[1]

# The Change-Resistant Organization

The same can be said for customer satisfaction measurement, and it carries the same hazard of techno-narcissism. Let's examine some of the ways that various members of a traditional, hierarchical organization can, at their worst, negatively impact an organizational shift toward customer satisfaction.

## Salespeople

There is a tendency for salespeople to be protective of *their* customers. Typically they don't want anybody else in the organization talking to them because knowledge about customers is the salesperson's power base and source of self esteem. Salespeople actually believe they know what their customers want, even though they don't know how to ask the right questions or listen for the answers. What salespeople do "know" usually isn't passed along in the form of data that can be examined using research disciplines and methods. It tends to be anecdotal and dogmatic. There is a concern, often legitimate, on the part of salespeople that if they reveal what they know about customers, management will start cutting commissions, gerrymandering sales territories, or turning the best business into house accounts. Incentive structures are usually designed to move the goods, not to satisfy and retain customers. Not being stupid, salespeople respond by spending their valuable time on pushing product, to the exclusion of all else. Cut any salesperson, and he or she bleeds price; they "know" the company could sell a lot more stuff if they would just get more competitive on pricing.

## Sales Managers

The pressure on sales managers is to make the numbers. They are paid accordingly, and that is how they get their "congrats" from top management. Their time is spent poring over sales numbers, to single out recalcitrant salespeople who need an arm around the shoulder and some advice on "how you succeed in this company." There isn't much time for getting out with customers to find out what is on their minds, and that is not an activity that gets much of a push from management except when some top executive returns from a trip agitated about a complaint heard from a customer. Sales managers occupy the hottest seat in the company. When sales are down, it's up to them to fix things, even though they have little or no control over most of the elements that influence sales. When sales are up and it's time to take credit, they have to stand in line behind the strategic thinkers and product geniuses. If they talk about deficiencies in the customer satisfaction area, it's often heard as a whining excuse for not doing their job of moving the goods. Small wonder they don't focus on customer satisfaction.

## Marketing

This is a world in which numbers act as surrogates for people. The god of market research lives in this Valhalla. The core beliefs here were nurtured in the school of mass marketing. Get enough numbers about demographics and psychographics, slice and dice them, overlay them on historical sales data, allocate resources cost-effectively, and voilá, you have a marketing plan. Marketing people spend infinitely more time with computer printouts than they do with the people who pay the bills, namely the customers. They are at severe risk of catching techno-narcissism. Despite the fact that the concept of marketing affects every aspect of business, marketing people tend to operate in a watertight compartment isolated from production, quality, finance, operations, customer service—even from sales at the front line. They prefer to keep themselves wrapped in a cocoon of professional mystique, not unlike scientists, engineers, and finance people. (And when sales turn sour, marketing people often maintain it's the result of an ineffective sales force. It didn't happen on their watch.)

## Executive Management

In many organizations, the executive world can be described as splendid isolation. Although many executives tell their subordinates with a straight face that they don't want surprises and consequently need to hear the bad news, the reality is, yes, they don't like surprises, but anybody who tells them an unpleasant truth is likely to get handed his or her head. Reward systems clearly favor the sycophant, so it's no wonder such behavior proliferates. In the executive boardroom, the voice of the customer is seldom heard; even when it is, it lacks the resonance of the voice at the head of the table. Whereas the isolation of the management suite is genteel and comfortable, the world of customers is contentious, demanding, messy, hard to understand. Is it any wonder that executives seldom venture into this hostile territory? When they make an occasional foray, should it be a surprise that they may not fully understand what they hear? Incentives for executives are usually linked to achievement of short-term goals—move the goods, make a buck, pump up the stock—not to customer retention and relationship building. In short, the executive environment can be inconsistent with the demands of organizational cultural change aimed at improving customer satisfaction.

## Finance

Chief financial officers bear a heavy burden. Not only are they supposed to exert control so nobody can cook the books, but they are supposed to make sure that the organization has the financial resources it needs at the most favorable rates possible, while at the same time helping to allocate precious resources for maximum bang for the buck. Most of the people who do this kind of work advance through the accounting ranks. They are concerned about trial closes, getting the numbers out within ever-tightening deadlines, cash flow, meeting the standards of auditors, and a host of data-handling considerations. It is difficult for people with these proclivities, in careers filled with arcane technical training, to accept the idea that customer satisfaction measurements are as important as, and perhaps more important than, operating statements and balance sheets. It's a leap into the unknown to think about customers, employees, knowledge, and learning capacity as the most important assets of an organization. How can they be assets when you can't put them on a balance sheet?

## Engineers/Scientists

If ever there were a group that considers itself apart and special, it is the engineers and scientists. In many organizations, the technical people have fostered the idea of dual career tracks, one for them and one for everybody else with more plebeian interests. The technical people take immense pride in knowledge that the uninitiated (everyone else in the organization) don't have. They love to fill their white boards with formulas that only they and their fellow cognoscenti can understand. When it comes to designing products or machinery, they barely tolerate ideas from outside the fraternity; after all, they are the masters of physics and chemistry. This has led to some of the worst-designed products imaginable, when viewed from the customer's perspective. For example, some of the early spacecraft controls had to be completely redesigned when the astronauts pointed out that the craft were essentially unflyable. The relatively new fields of human-factors engineering and ergonomics have resulted from customers nudging their way into a world where they were not welcome in the past.

## Production

Ever since Frederick Taylor established the basic concepts of industrial engineering and Henry Ford developed the assembly line into a marvel of efficiency and productivity, production has had as its driving force to make things faster, cheaper, better. The assembly worker has been a check-your-brains-at-the-door component of a big, noisy machine. The only way to be sure the frail, human part of the system was working was by watching like a hawk and inspecting quality at each step of the process. It wasn't deemed important for production workers—a replaceable commodity—to know anything about customers. Sometimes factory workers did not even know the end use of the gizmo they produced. One of the precepts of the quality movement, when it began taking hold in the post-World War II period, was that quality could not be "inspected in." Since then, production workers have had a nose in the tent of customer satisfaction but have rarely been full partners with the other functional areas of business when it comes to listening and responding to the voice of the customer.

## Customer Service/Field Service

Until recently, these functions were viewed by most organizations as overhead, a necessary evil. Management wanted them kept to a cost-effective minimum, achieving a delicate balance between cost control and not losing customers by abusing them. It's easy to imagine the mindset and behavior patterns of employees who well realize how poorly their function is considered. This has begun to change somewhat in recent years as companies realize that they can charge for service and make money doing so. The service contract has become the weapon of choice. In some cases, service is so expensive a function that companies have simply abandoned it, choosing to encourage a do-it-yourself or replacement mentality. Customer service departments are treated as an appendage, not part of the corpus of the business. Rarely do they have direct access to top management and a seat at the table when important decisions are being made. Only in exceptional cases do companies think of product and service as bundled components of a total customer relationship that should drive decision making. Yet customer service departments are on the receiving end of immensely valuable information. For the most part it stays right there, unappreciated and not acted upon.

## Department Isolation

Too often, these functions stand in their companies like separate silos in an Iowa cornfield. Nothing moves between them. Each department is privy to its own information; there is no incentive to share and no methods for doing so. The culture and incentives that drive each department individually mitigate against understanding and responding to customers.

# The Pro-Change Organization

Contrast this with an organization carefully designed to use customer satisfaction measurement as its nervous system. The organization is flat ("delayered," to use the parlance of the day). There is organizational telemetry—customer satisfaction measurement—operating in every functional area of the business. Incentives are firmly in place at all levels of the organization to reward improvements in customer satisfaction and customer retention. When the organizational telemetry signals a variance needing attention, enough data are at hand for management by fact.

The total composite customer satisfaction picture is presented at meetings where all functional areas of the business are represented and heard. Differences of viewpoint are openly expressed, and welcomed. Solutions are negotiated by cross-functional teams so that diverse interests are always represented.

The organizational culture has been carefully developed in an environment in which there is a shared vision of being customer-centered. The culture is insistent that the question always asked at decision-making time is, "What is best for the customer?" There is a quiet confidence that the organization will continue to be successful because it is aligned to principles that are right and virtually failure proof. Instead of constituting a series of obstacles to overcome, the organizational structure facilitates and supports the efforts of everyone to improve customer satisfaction.

Leaders who mean it when they say they want a customer-centered organization can achieve their goal only after aligning the organizational structure with that purpose. Significant transformational change department by department, function by function—is usually required. The challenge involved in making such significant changes is formidable, but worth the effort and stress.

# Reference

1. "Editorial," *Business Week* (June 26, 1995), p. 154.

# 6

# Strategic Planning

Strategic planning, without good customer satisfaction information, is like designing a stadium without knowing what game is to be played there. After you find out whether it is baseball, football, hockey, soccer, or basketball, there is a lot of costly reconfiguring to do.

When executives troop off to the mountaintop for their annual strategic planning exercise, they often end up with *operational* planning rather than *strategic* planning. But what is worse yet is that the discussion usually centers around internal considerations.

The atmosphere is permeated by a macho mentality that shouts, "We're in charge. We can go wherever we want to go. Now let's decide the best way to dominate our industry and flay our competitors."

One popular book on strategic planning maintains that "strategic thinking is the process of thought that goes on inside the head of the CEO and the key people around him or her."[1] That is a typical, internally oriented, egocentric mindset. The same book barely mentions customers and doesn't even give a tip of the hat to customer satisfaction measurement.

How different it is when the thought process revolves around what is going on in the minds and hearts of customers! The discussion then is more likely to center on how to do a better job of serving customers than how to gain percentage points of market share. There is ample evidence that market share and profitability take care of themselves at companies that achieve high customer satisfaction ratings.[2]

At a typical strategic planning retreat a number of years ago, Motorola executives spent hours talking about strategy, market share, new products, and so on. Finally, the vice president of marketing screwed up his courage and said something to the effect, "We're not talking about what matters. Our customers think our products are junk. We're not going anywhere until we fix our quality."

From that point on, the meeting was up for grabs. They literally tore up the script and started over. The result was an unrelenting drive for quality that has made the name Motorola synonymous with the term Six Sigma Quality, the organization a Baldrige Award winner, and the corporation highly successful and profitable.

# Traditional Strategic Planning in a Vacuum

There is a reason why strategic planning meetings function in a vacuum, unpenetrated by the customer: Most companies don't know their customers very well. They lack the answers to the obvious questions that would be asked if the spotlight of strategic planning attention were directed on the customer.

To be sure, when the talk turns to marketing and sales the usual tiresome list of customer wants and needs is generated. But this talk lacks substance, backup data, sound research. Its basis is often the dogmatic attitude that "we know what our customers want." Unless there is the support of a comprehensive customer satisfaction measurement *system*, that is likely to be a hollow claim.

A marketing vice president at a company noted for product innovation concedes: "We don't really know what our customers' lives are like, how they feel about us, what motivates them. Frankly we don't talk to them. Our focus has always been on our distributors. We're beginning to realize that that isn't good enough. We're finding out that the competitors who are nipping at our heels are spending a lot of time with customers. They're beginning to get results."

## Profit Impact of Market Strategy

A number of strategic planning fads have captured the fancy of executives over the years. One of them was PIMS, the profit impact of market strategy. PIMS researchers compiled an Everest of operating data on hundreds of companies, looking for common denominators among the most successful.

Not surprisingly, it turned out that there was a correlation between market share and profitability. Thus was born the school of strategic planning single-mindedly devoted to market share. One of the devotees was GE, which, as we have seen, openly declared its determination to be first or second in every market in which it competed. Also-ran products and divisions were jettisoned.

There is nothing wrong with paying attention to market share, as long as it is put in perspective. It is important to remember that market share results from satisfying customers. Market share is in fact a customer satisfaction measurement.

Unfortunately, marketing data get undeserved respect because they seem to come from some mysterious digital netherworld. The problem is the data are undefiled by human experience. Planners often forget that the data they are dealing with are a surrogate for business reality, and historical at that.

## Strategic Business Units

There was and continues to be a strategic planning emphasis on strategic business units (SBUs). The idea is to break the company into discrete components and select strategies most appropriate to each unit's situation. Companies then can be thought of as a portfolio of individual businesses.

In today's business environment, there is a whole lot wrong with the SBU way of looking at companies:

- It is an internal focus. How should we organize, staff, budget, and manage our SBU in order to shine among the other SBUs and get management's blessing? The result of thinking in such terms is that organizational energy flows to these issues instead of being focused externally on customers.
- Top management begins to look at SBUs as pawns in a chess game: Move them, sacrifice them, do whatever it takes to win the game. Management tends to learn a lot about acquisitions and mergers, but not much about how to grow a company by responding to customers.
- SBUs breed the idea of profit centers. Peter Drucker put that idea to bed when he wrote, "Many, many years ago, I coined the term 'profit center.' I am thoroughly ashamed of it now, because inside a business there are no profit centers, just cost centers. Profit comes only from the outside. When a customer returns with a repeat order and his check doesn't bounce, you have a profit center."[3]
- Opportunities don't fit neatly within SBU boundaries. Where the SBU idea is in full flower, the competency does not exist to

work horizontally across boundaries; as a result, the company's most significant opportunities are likely to be missed.
- Customer satisfaction information does not flow well across organizational boundaries, even those within an SBU, much less corporatewide. Information often is pigeonholed, suppressed, or ignored, while management is preoccupied with its organizational chess board.

## Focus on the Driving Force

Another strategic planning concept revolves around the idea of identifying the driving force in your business and then building on it. For example, companies can be driven primarily by product, market, technology, capacity, growth, profit, distribution methods, natural resources, or anything else.

In his book *Strategy Pure and Simple*, Michel Robert makes this observation: "The essence of strategic thinking is the CEO's and management's clear understanding of which component of the business is more important than all others and is the 'heartbeat' of the business and, as such, lends itself more to certain products, customers, market segments, and geographic markets."[4]

The customer is never identified as the "heartbeat." Instead, advocates of this planning approach proffer an off-hand acknowledgment that the customer is an important strategic element, regardless of the driving force identified. The problem here is one of emphasis. Preoccupation with a driving force can dilute attention to the customer.

An example of a distribution-driven company was Sears. Its move into real estate and financial services was a clear attempt to capitalize on its distribution reach. It didn't work very well. Meanwhile, Wal-Mart focused on the customer and was able to challenge Sears for dominance in retailing.

# Customer-Centered Strategic Planning

A company that identifies customers as the driving force has a clarity of purpose that cuts through a lot of strategic planning complexity. Such a company taps a wellspring of ideas for new products and services, opens up new territories and alliances, stimulates innovation, encourages flexibility, and keeps the company on its toes.

The difference is between internal and external points of view. A typical driving-force kind of planning exercise revolves around the idea, "This is the kind of company we are. Let's stay focused and get better at it." A customer-focused approach to planning says, "What would make life better for our customers and how can we build our company around that?"

Bring up the subject of how the customer fits into strategic planning, and somebody will opine that customers don't know what they want. The critic offers several examples to prove the point. The usual ones are that customers didn't know they wanted fax machines, compact discs, and automated teller machines before such things were developed. This looks like a potent argument for dismissing the customer from the planing process.

But the people-don't-know-what-they-want idea betrays a remarkable ignorance of what is happening in leading-edge companies. One of them is Sony, whose visionary leader Akio Morita puts a different spin on the fact that people may not be able to articulate what they want: "Our plan is to lead the public with new products rather than ask them what kind of products they want. The public does not know what is possible, but we do."[5]

In *Competing for the Future,* Gary Hamel and C. K. Prahalad explain: "There are three kinds of companies. Companies that try to lead customers where they don't want to go (these are companies that find the idea of being customer-led an insight); companies that listen to customers and then respond to their articulated needs (needs that are probably already being satisfied by more foresightful competitors); and companies that lead customers where they want to go, but don't know it yet."[6]

Two aspects of a deeply ingrained commitment to customers lead to industry foresight. The organizational telemetry of customer satisfaction measurement alerts and sensitizes the whole organization to what is happening in the customer's world. Second, this in turn stimulates empathy with basic human needs. "As much as anything," Hamel and Prahalad write, "foresight comes from really wanting to make a difference in people's lives." They continue:

"Although potentially useful, technology forecasting, market research, scenario planning, and competitor analysis won't necessarily yield industry foresight. None of these tools compels senior management to reconceive the corporation and the industries in which it competes. Only by changing the lens through which the corporation is viewed (core competencies versus strategic business units), only by changing the lens through which markets are viewed (functionalities versus products), only by cleaning off the accumulated grime on the lens (seeing with a child's eyes), only by peering through multiple lenses (eclecticism), and only by occasionally disbelieving what one actually sees (challenging price-performance conventions, thinking like a contrarian) can the future be anticipated."[7]

# Strategic Listening

It would be a good idea to give everyone who is about to attend a strategic planning meeting an assignment beforehand: Spend a week on the road, visiting customers. Get some windshield time with the sales force. But before departing on an excursion like that, everyone should be given training in listening and observing skills. Then, at the start of the strategic planning meeting, everyone should be asked to report on what they learned.

A facilitator can capture the essence of each report as it is delivered and, by means of factor analysis, condense the findings into groupings of core ideas. These ideas can then be explored in the context of strategic planning. This assures that the stew of the meeting is flavored with the spice of the customer.

If a directive is issued to spend a week with clients, protests rise in chorus. People complain that they don't have the time, that it will take them away from their work. The whole purpose, of course, is to help them realize that listening to clients *is* their work.

The discipline of market research should be linked to the art of listening. Each has strengths and weaknesses. Together, used as a validity check on each other, they are more likely to arrive at the truth. Listening, of course, is subject to the errors that necessarily creep in from small sample size and the biases of both interviewer and respondent. Research often is flawed by its narrow focus ("Do you prefer red or black?").

Many people are not very good at listening. There is a tendency to hear what you want to hear and to filter everything through your own belief system. The good listener is open to different points of view and tries hard, in an uncritical, unquestioning way, to be empathetic. These are not qualities that have been highly regarded and developed in the business world.

Researchers, on the other hand, get so enthralled by the beauty of their algorithms, regressions, charts, and graphs that they can lose touch with the human factor and the goals and objectives of the organizations they work for. There is always a risk that they do not see the forest for the trees.

A customer satisfaction measurement system should be designed to bring in information from multiple sources (listening and research), validate and analyze the information, and arrive at balanced conclusions amenable to action.

In advance of strategic planning meetings (well in advance), it would be helpful if executives asked these questions:

- Can we say with confidence that we really know and understand our customers?
- Do we have systems in place for validating and cross-checking customer satisfaction measurement data?
- Have we undergone the kind of cultural change needed to make our entire organization customer-centered?
- Have the people who are invited to this meeting spent enough time with customers recently to be current and empathetic about what life is like for our customers?
- Is our planning going to be based on well-researched and analyzed data, and not merely on opinion and anecdotal examples?
- Are we prepared intellectually and emotionally to buy into the Baldrige criteria, which put the customer in the driver's seat?
- Are our strategic planning format and methodology designed around the customer?

# References

1. Michel Robert, *Strategy Pure and Simple* (New York: McGraw-Hill, 1993).
2. Richard C. Whitely, *The Customer-Driven Company* (Reading, Mass.: Addison Wesley, 1991), p. 201.
3. *ASAP*, *Forbes* (August 29, 1994), p. 107.
4. Michel Robert, *Strategy Pure and Simple*.
5. Gary Hamel and C. K. Prahalad, *Competing for the Future* (Boston: Harvard Business School Press, 1994), p. 100.
6. Ibid.
7. Ibid., p. 105.

# Part Two

# CURRENT

# APPROACHES

Few would argue with the observations of opinion leaders, futurists, academics, and journalists that we are living through a dramatic reordering of society. Various labels have been applied, most notably *paradigm shift*. In the business world, turmoil and uncertainty have given birth to various coping concepts: total quality management, business process reengineering, the learning organization, teams, organizational transformation, and new concepts of leadership.

In one way or another, each of these concepts plays a role in the overarching idea of putting customer concerns at the heart of an organization. In order to complete a shift from conventional business and organizational practices to the reality of being truly customer-centered, it helps for all involved to see the linkage between currently popular management ideas and the world of work that is emerging in the twenty-first century. That linkage is explored in the chapters of Part Two.

# 7

# Historical Perspective

The business world is in the midst of a renaissance. Just as Europe emerged from medieval darkness by rediscovering arts and literature, business is rediscovering customers. In many ways, the new focus on customers is a return to how customers were served by artisans and storekeepers in simpler times.

Just as the idea of the Renaissance man, a person whose interests span many and diverse fields of knowledge, was central to revival five hundred years ago, today's business leader must move beyond mastery of a few technical disciplines to a broad understanding of the complexities of human behavior.

These thoughts may have the musty odor of academia about them, but they have practical, down-to-earth application in today's fast-paced, rapidly changing, often hostile, and competitive business environment. A single, meaning-packed phrase is at the heart of this idea. It is customer satisfaction measurement.

## How We Got off Track

How did business get so far off the track that a renaissance became necessary? The answers are mass production, mass communication, mass marketing, and World War II. The idea of producing and selling things in large, standardized quantities, promoted by mass media advertising, became the dominant business strategy after the war. In the postwar period, when people had lots of money and an insatiable appetite for goods, it was easy to sell virtually anything you could make.

Compared to today, it was relatively easy being an executive during that epoch. Mastery of balance sheets and spreadsheets was valued at a premium. Business was conducted in the soft glow of the overhead projector.

Finally, in the late 1970s, the long-abused, benighted consumer rebelled, cheered on by fast-moving competitors. Big, out-of-touch companies stumbled and in some cases fell. In reaction, a huge industry grew up to service business's new preoccupation with the idea that quality was important to success.

At the same time, management fads and panaceas abounded, beginning with the publication of *In Search of Excellence* in 1982. For a while, the focus was on marketing; then on finance, then human resources, then technology, downsizing and reengineering, and human development.

Now the realization has dawned that it is time to go back to where it all began, with a sincere desire to know, understand, and serve customers.

We noted it earlier, but it bears repeating, as Jack Smith, the CEO of General Motors said it succinctly: "Focus everything—all assets, all decisions—on your customers. They are the ultimate arbiters of success or failure."

# The Birth of
# Customer Satisfaction Measurement

Peter Drucker, along with others, is also a proponent of the concept that you can't manage what you can't measure. He asserts that measurement is one of the five key functions of managers. Indeed, the idea of measurement is fundamental to the scientific method, and it is arguably the bedrock of human knowledge. The nineteenth-century physicist Lord Kelvin is reputed to have said that if you can't measure something, you don't understand it.

In retrospect, there seems to be an inevitability to the convergence of interest in customers and a desire to measure what customers think, feel, and do. It is surprising how slow it has been in coming, and how elemental it still is in many companies. Even some of the biggest, best, most resourceful companies are only now beginning to develop full-blown customer satisfaction measurement systems.

Perhaps the mercurial, complex nature of human beings is intimidating to technically trained business executives who thrive on the seeming certitude of numbers. Perhaps the residual strength in traditional hierarchical organization structures is still getting in the way. Perhaps the new art and science of customer satisfaction measurement has yet to earn its spurs.

Many are surprised at how recent the concept of CSM is. It first moved beyond the realm of occasional ad hoc marketing research studies in the early 1970s, when AT&T introduced SAM (satisfaction attitude measurement), an ongoing mail survey of customers who had experienced a recent service call. Eventually this program was converted to a telephone methodology called TELSAM, a large, continuous-measurement program involving hundreds of thousands of interviews and running into millions of dollars.

TELSAM set the stage for the aggressive pursuit of satisfaction measurement programs by marketing research companies. An early internal use of CSM was via customer feedback cards, for example the cards on tables in restaurants or hotels. Another early CSM application was mystery shopping performance measurement, using evaluators who pretended to be customers.

In recent years, CSM has matured as a specialization within companies and consulting firms. It is not uncommon now for companies to have a vice president of customer satisfaction. A number of consulting firms concentrate on the field, and several universities are pursuing academic research within the discipline. A body of knowledge is growing rapidly, supported by books and other publications.

CSM got another boost in the form of the American customer satisfaction index (ACSI), a new economic indicator that measures customer evaluations of the quality of goods and services purchased in the United States.

# The American Customer Satisfaction Index (ACSI)

The ACSI was developed by the National Quality Research Center at the University of Michigan School of Business Administration, with financial support from the American Society of Quality Control.

The idea behind the ACSI is to provide useful information on quality to complement present measures of the U.S. economy such as the consumer price index and the index of buying intentions. Claes Fornell, the University of Michigan professor who led the ACSI design team, explained, "When a buyer recognizes quality, it is reflected in customer satisfaction. Customer satisfaction, in turn, can lead to increased revenue. Customers are an economic asset. They're not on the balance sheet but they should be."[1]

When the ACSI was first released in October 1994, it began lending respectability to an idea that is only just beginning to permeate the financial management circles populated by CFOs, controllers, and CPAs. The idea was summed up by Prof. Robert Simons of Harvard Graduate School when he wrote: "Traditional financial indicators must be augmented by new diagnostic measures that monitor market-based variables such as quality and customer satisfaction. These nonfinancial measures, which focus attention on customers, key internal processes, and innovation, are an important step in the right direction."[2]

The ACSI has been released quarterly since 1994. It answers such questions as:

- Does the U.S. economy reflect improvement in customer satisfaction with goods and services, or is the quality of economic output, as evaluated by customers, declining?
- How does the change in ACSI compare with changes in the consumer price index, and to changes in productivity, employment, corporate profits, balance of trade, and the gross domestic product?

The concept of an index results in a useful tool, especially when the research is conducted continuously to identify changes and trends.

The ACSI compares one industry to another. For example, how does manufacturing compare to retail, in the eyes of the customer? But the data become more significant over time by showing changes in the relative scores of industries, indicating improvement or decline.

## Customer Satisfaction Index

A better known index is the approach used widely in the auto industry. Manufacturers regularly survey customers by way of dealers on their degree of satisfaction with both product and services. The auto companies provide their dealers with customer satisfaction index (CSI) scores showing how well they are doing compared with other dealers, locally and nationally.

The auto industry puts muscle into its CSIs by rewarding dealers financially for doing well or punishing them in various ways for substandard performance.

A number of companies have developed CSI approaches that help divisions, departments, or other organizational entities keep score of their customer satisfaction performance. The ones that have been most successful carefully guard against using CSI data punitively against employees or managers.

# The Connection Between Service and Satisfaction

During the formative years of the global quality movement, the emphasis was on product quality. Thus the burden has rested most heavily on production and engineering. Gradually, the emphasis is shifting to service in recognition that sources of customer dissatisfaction most often have nothing to do with the product. They fall in some other area of customer relationships.

Earl Naumann explained in *Creating Customer Value:* "From the customer's perspective, product quality and service quality are virtually inseparable. Delivering high-service quality is now absolutely essential to creating good customer value. Due to the rapidly changing technological environment, service quality now holds more potential for creating a competitive advantage than does product quality. But delivering service quality may be even more difficult than improving product quality."[3]

Recognizing this, alert and far-sighted leaders of organizations—business, nonprofit and governmental—are ushering in a new era in which customer satisfaction measurement is destined to play a vital role.

# References

1. *1994 American Customer Satisfaction Index,* pamphlet published by ASQC and University of Michigan, 1994.
2. Robert Simons, "Strategy, Control, and the CFO," *CFO* (December 1994), p. 12.
3. Earl Naumann, *Creating Customer Value* (Cincinnati, Ohio: Thomson Executive Press, 1995).

# 8

# Quality

The simple idea that the customer decides what quality is represents both a boon to customer satisfaction and a barrier. The quality idea got management's attention long before customer satisfaction was being discussed seriously. Quality opened the door and customer satisfaction tip-toed in behind it.

Unfortunately, in many organizations quality is perceived as a project with a beginning and an end. At some point, management thinks of it as having been accomplished, and no longer a pressing issue. If customer satisfaction is tightly linked to quality it can get tarred with the same brush.

In fact the quality world currently is undergoing a period of angst that has produced a good deal of introspection. Quality professionals complain that they seem to have lost the attention of top management. They see their departments being thinned or even eliminated through downsizing. Customer satisfaction, when thought of in the same terms as quality, can suffer the same fate.

Illustrating this point, a senior quality engineer at a very progressive Fortune 500 company told a consultant that it would be a waste of time to make a presentation on customer satisfaction capabilities to the company's quality council. The people on the quality council, he explained, no longer had management's ear.

On reflection, management's relative lack of interest in quality is understandable. Quality often is equated with products, engineering, and production. These are not big issues at that particular company. Technically, their products are the best in the world by any standard. Management has other priorities to be concerned about. The engineer's advice to the consultant was to make a customer satisfaction presentation to the general manager's council—that is, to people who can make decisions.

It is sad testimony to the rigidity of the authority structure in many organizations that all of the decision making that really matters is at the top. There is talk of empowerment, but it is farcical. Nobody makes decisions without getting approval, either explicit or tacit.

In authoritarian organizations, it's easy for people to hide from responsibility. If you don't have to make decisions, you don't have to think. There are no choices, no issues, no dilemmas, no paradoxes. It's very easy to say, "I'll check on it." "I'll run it up the line." "I'll get a sign off."

In a perverse way, the emergence of teams has made matters worse. Now even the bosses can sidestep responsibility. They buck the tough decisions to a team and wait, often interminably, for a consensus. The impression is inescapable that in some organizations nobody makes decisions; choices emerge mysteriously as if from the ether.

Obviously there are benefits to involving people in the decision-making process, benefits to collaboration and interchanges of communication. But it is important to recognize that there can be too much of a good thing. Everyone in an organization needs to take on responsibility. There can be no sense of responsibility without the freedom to make decisions and take action.

The model for effective decision making exists, and ironically it is a fundamental precept of the quality movement. It was articulated by the late W. Edwards Deming, who many consider to be the spiritual leader of the quality movement. The answer is there for those who would see it, but the message has been muted by its sheer familiarity. In many cases, management has grown weary of the importunings of quality engineers. Instead, executives would do well to revisit quality, viewing it in its broadest terms, including customer satisfaction as the driver.

# The Human Factor of Deming's Quality

Quality is often thought of as a technical matter. The idea is reinforced by the Pareto charts, histograms, scatter diagrams, and statistical process control charts that quality engineers love to display. Although Deming was trained as a statistician and had a healthy respect for measurement, it was barely mentioned in his famed Fourteen Points and Seven Deadly Diseases (see Appendixes A and B). Instead, his Point Eleven is *eliminate numerical quotas*. Quotas take into account only numbers, he said, not quality or methods. They are usually a guarantee of inefficiency and high cost. To hold a job, a person meets a quota at any cost, without regard to damage to his company.

Deming addressed the issue of responsibility with Point Eight: *Drive out fear*. Many employees are afraid to ask questions or take a position, he said, even when they do not understand what their job is or what is right or wrong. They continue to do things the wrong way, or not do them at all. The economic losses from fear are appalling. To ensure better quality and productivity, it is necessary that people, workers and managers alike, feel secure. How many executives go to the office thinking, "What can I do today to help drive out fear?"

Again focusing on the human issues, Deming created Point Twelve: *Remove barriers to pride of workmanship*. People are eager to do a good job, he said, and distressed when they cannot. Too often, misguided supervisors, faulty equipment, and defective materials stand in the way of good performance. These barriers must be removed.

Deming was swimming against the stream when he listed as one of the Seven Deadly Diseases *evaluation by performance, merit rating, or annual review of performance*. The effects of these almost ubiquitous management tools, in his view, are devastating: Teamwork is destroyed, rivalry is nurtured. Performance ratings, he contended, build fear and leave people bitter, despondent, beaten. They also encourage defection in the ranks of management.

He also disparaged *running a company on visible figures alone* (disease number five). His message is that the most important figures are unknown and unknowable—the multiplier effect of a happy customer, for example.

Deming had a healthy respect for customers. His confidante, Mary Walton, wrote in *Deming Management at Work*:

> The quality effort requires a new way of thinking about the customer, and thinking as well about new customers. Spoiled by decades of success, when customers accepted whatever companies produced, American managers have yet to grasp that they *must* satisfy customer needs, because if they don't their competitor will. With the customer as the reference point, priorities become easier to set.
>
> In quality-minded organizations, the word "customer" describes more than a relationship in which money merely changes hands. It describes the exchange of services as well. For any given enterprise, there are two sets of customers: external and internal.

The external customer is the end user of a product or service. The internal customer is the person or work unit that receives the product or the service of another within the same company.

Too often one department does not understand how its work is used by the next, and thus cannot learn what things are important in carrying out its tasks. The notion of internal customers lends relevance to each employee's job and is absolutely critical to a quality transformation.[1]

# Return on Quality

The linkage between quality and customer is at the root of a new movement known as ROQ, return on quality. Its devotees believe in calculating the cost of quality initiatives, determining what key factors retain customers, and focusing on quality efforts most likely to improve customer satisfaction at a reasonable cost. The final tenet of ROQ is to improve programs continuously, measuring results against anticipated gains.

This would have warmed Deming's heart. He decried that "Americans are accustomed to seeing work projects in a linear fashion, with a beginning and end. The job is done; on to the next. Continuous or never-ending improvement requires instead a circular approach." Deming advocated working on processes rather than specific tasks or problems. "Processes by their nature can never be solved but only improved," he believed. "In working on processes, one does, of course, solve some problems."[2]

The ROQ movement was fueled by total quality management horror stories. In a cover story on "Making Quality Pay," *Business Week* came to this conclusion:

> Rare today is the chief executive who does not profess to be an enthusiastic convert to the goal of improving quality. Manufacturers were the first to join the "total quality management," or TQM, bandwagon, but they were soon followed by banks, telephone companies, and hospitals. Even local governments have embraced quality as they try to boost "customer" satisfaction with public services.
>
> The problem is, so many private and public organizations are pursuing quality in a hidebound way—by following the dictates of their bureaucracies and management hierarchies rather than by listening to their customers. Yet the evidence is undeniable: TQM only works when a company finds out what customers really care

about. Do they want on-time performance? Personal service and some hand-holding? Or a cheaper price for a stripped-down product? The answer is not always obvious, unless companies ask customers the right questions and then painfully overhaul their operations to respond efficiently to customer demands.[3]

Federal Express, a 1990 recipient of the coveted Baldrige National Quality Award, was offered by *Business Week* as an example of a customer-inspired, painful overhaul. In its sorting operation, FedEx stressed speed over accuracy. Workers met schedules, but the number of misdirected packages soared as they scrambled to meet deadlines. The issue proved so important from the customer's point of view that FedEx has invested $100 million in new equipment that efficiently and accurately routes packages to various destinations.

Robert E. Allen, CEO of AT&T, insists on quarterly reports from each of the company's fifty-three business units that spell out quality improvements and their subsequent financial impact. Making clear that he doesn't see the quality movement as transitory, Allen says, "The renaissance in quality will go on as long as the original Renaissance, which lasted two hundred years."[4]

Appreciation of the importance of quality has come a long way since a Gallup survey in 1989 found that while 57 percent of boards of directors discuss quality of products and services regularly, 35 percent discuss quality only sometimes, rarely, or never. Service firms, according to Gallup, lagged industrial firms in knowledge of and degree of involvement in quality assurance activities and strategies.

Measuring ROQ is dicey at best. As Deming observed nearly a decade ago, faith in visible numbers should be tempered by the fact that the most important numbers are unknown and unknowable. What is the financial impact of knowing what customers value and then giving it to them in spades?

Michael Treacy and Fred Wiersema, in their book *The Discipline of Market Leaders,* contend that companies can't succeed by trying to be all things to all people. Instead, they should find the unique value that they alone can deliver to the marketplace. That value should be something customers want. "Customers today want more of those things they value," according to the authors. "If they value low cost, they want it lower. If they value convenience or speed when they buy, they want it easier and faster. If they look for state-of-the-art design, they want to see the art pushed forward. If they need expert advice, they want companies to give them more depth, more time, and more of a feeling that they're the only customer."[5]

The authors ask plaintively, "Why do some companies endear themselves to us while others just don't seem to know how to please? Don't the latter see what they are doing—and not doing? How long do they think they can get away with it? No one goes to work in the morning intending to fail. But managers at a great many companies, for all practical purposes, have chosen failure. Don't they see that the world has changed?"

Treacy and Wiersema offer these tantalizing examples:

- Why can Casio sell a calculator more cheaply than Kellogg can sell a box of corn flakes? Does corn cost that much more than silicon?
- Why does it take only a few minutes and no paperwork to pick up or drop off a rental car at Hertz's #1 Club Gold, but twice that time and an annoying name/address form to check into a Hilton hotel? Are they afraid you'll steal the room?
- Why is it that Federal Express can "absolutely, positively" deliver a package overnight, but Delta, American, and United Airlines have trouble keeping your bags on your plane? Do they think you don't care?
- Why does Lands' End remember your last order and your family members' sizes, but after ten years of membership you are still being solicited by American Express to join? Don't the people at Amex know you're a customer?
- Why can you get patient help from a Home Depot clerk when selecting a $2.70 package of screws, but you can't get any advice when purchasing a $2,700 personal computer from IBM's direct-ordering service? Doesn't IBM think customer service is worth the time?

The single answer to all of these questions goes back to the basic precept of the quality movement: The customer decides what quality is. Find out what the customer wants and values, utilizing the techniques and technology of organizational telemetry or customer satisfaction measurement. Then foster an organizational culture that can respond to the signals emanating from the organizational telemetry.

## The Customer-Intimate Company

Treacy and Wiersema offer this model of what they call a "customer-intimate" company. The model is not so different from what Deming said:

- An obsession with helping the customer understand exactly what's needed, and ensuring the solution gets implemented properly.
- A business structure that delegates decision making to employees who are close to the customer.
- Management systems that are geared toward creating results for carefully selected and nurtured clients.
- A culture that embraces specific rather than general solutions and thrives on deep and lasting client relationships.[6]

These laudable goals cannot be achieved without the direct involvement of upper management. Unfortunately, senior level executives traditionally delegate the management of quality instead of becoming directly involved. First quality was delegated to the chief inspector; with later enlightenment, quality was handed over to the quality manager.

Companies that have attained leadership in quality are led by executives who took charge instead of delegating. They established goals, provided resources, participated in training, and championed reward and recognition systems. And they did it personally.

It seems paradoxical that the path to quality, and hence customer satisfaction and success in the marketplace, requires the empowerment of employees at all levels of an organization, while at the same time demanding the attention and involvement of executives. It also seems paradoxical that the quality movement is undergoing stressful reevaluation in the minds of executives at the same time that one of its basic precepts, the all-important role of the customer, is moving to the forefront.

But, after all, living with paradox is intrinsic to intelligence and executive leadership.

# References

1. Mary Walton, *Deming Management at Work* (New York: G. P. Putnam, 1990).
2. Ibid., p. 21
3. David Greising, "Making Quality Pay," *Business Week* (August 8, 1994), p. 80.
4. Ibid.
5. Michael Treacy and Fred Wiersema, *The Discipline of Market Leaders* (Reading, Mass.: Addison-Wesley, 1995).
6. W. Edwards Deming, *Out of the Crisis* (Cambridge, Mass.: Center for Advanced Engineering Study, Massachusetts Institute of Technology, 1986). (See also Appendixes A and B in this book.)

# 9

# Reengineering

Three books that have imparted new meaning to the term "business best-seller": *In Search of Excellence* by Tom Peters and Robert Waterman, *The 7 Habits of Highly Effective People* by Stephen Covey, and *Reengineering the Corporation* by Michael Hammer and James Champy.

All three are self-help books for business. They share the premise that the old ways aren't working very well in today's fast-changing environment. Change, the authors say very persuasively, is not a choice; it is an imperative. *In Search of Excellence* identifies the characteristics of successful companies so they can be imitated. *The 7 Habits* does much the same with regard to individuals. *Reengineering* tells how to wipe the slate clean and start over.

Hammer and Champy buttress their arguments in behalf of reengineering with this statement: "Three forces, separately and in combination, are driving today's companies deeper and deeper into territory that most of their executives and managers find frighteningly unfamiliar. We call these forces the three Cs: Customers, Competition, and Change."[1]

All three factors are deeply involved in what it takes to be a customer-centered organization and are at the core of the message of this book. Disciplined use of customer satisfaction measurement can eliminate the words "frighteningly unfamiliar" as a description of the state of mind of executives and managers.

## Customers

The customer, as viewed by Hammer and Champy, is a different kind of creature in the 1990s. They explain, "Customers—consumers and corporations alike—demand products and services designed for their unique and particular needs. There is no longer any such notion as *the* customer; there is only *this* customer, the one with whom a seller is dealing at the moment and who now has the capacity to indulge his or her own personal tastes. The mass market has broken into pieces, some as small as a single customer."[2]

How did this untidy development occur? Here is the explanation in *Reengineering the Corporation*:

> Since the early 1980s, in the United States and other developed countries, the dominant force in the seller-customer relationship has shifted. Sellers no longer have the upper hand; customers do. Customers now tell suppliers what they want, when they want it, how they want it, and what they will pay. This new situation is unsettling to companies that have known life only in the mass market.
>
> In reality, a mass market never existed, but for most of this century the *idea* of the mass market provided manufacturers and service providers—from Henry Ford's car company to Thomas Watson's computer company—with the useful fiction that their customers were more or less alike. If that were true, or if buyers behaved as if it were true, then companies could assume that a standard product or service—a black car or a big blue computer—would satisfy most of them. Even those that weren't satisfied would buy what was offered, because they had little choice. Mass market suppliers in the United States had relatively few competitors, most of which offered very similar products and services. In fact, most consumers weren't dissatisfied. They didn't know that anything better or different was available.[3]

# Competition

Although capitalism places competition on a throne of reverence, there is perhaps no other factor causing executives more sleepless nights and Excedrin headaches. Just when all of the elegant machinery of corporate planning is beginning to mesh, along comes a competitor with an innovation the planners had never considered. As an example, while the big computer companies were savaging each other, but nonetheless growing rapidly and living in the lap of luxury, a couple of guys out on the West Coast dreamed up the personal computer, named it after a fruit, and changed the world forever.

Hammer and Champy write, "Start-up companies that carry no

organizational baggage and are not constrained by their histories can enter a market with the next product or service generation before existing companies can even recoup their development costs on the last one. Every established company today needs to post a lookout for start-ups."[4]

A different kind of example: There seemed nothing more monolithically powerful in this world than the big three automakers, known with geographical inaccuracy as "Detroit." Then the *keiretsus* over in Japan came up with the audacious idea that they could be major players in the world market for cars—starting in, of all places, the United States. They found Detroit's Achilles heel: quality.

And another: While Ma Bell sat serenely atop the telecommunications world, the government decided that parent AT&T was looking too much like a monopoly. The breakup of AT&T not only splintered a company, it splintered an entire industry. Enter MCI, Sprint, and legions of smaller companies. The telecommunications industry is now a free-for-all. No Marquis of Queensberry rules.

Conversely, competition for the corner grocer and shopkeeper has come in the form of huge, multi-tentacled enterprises that can afford to build and stock supermarkets and acreage-eating category-killer stores that offer customers variety, low cost, and convenience. The most successful now even beat the local merchants when it comes to customer service.

# Change

Twenty-five years ago, the editor of *Scientific American* was traveling around the country speaking to corporate executives about change. He was a kind of technological Paul Revere, sounding the alert about how change was accelerating.

The magazine had graphed the pace of change from the beginning of recorded history, tracking such things as energy utilization, the speed of travel, productivity, the extent of human knowledge, population, efficiency of farming, and the number of inventions. On a logarithmic graph, all of the lines were horizontal and virtually flat for millennia. The movement was almost imperceptible until the twentieth century.

Then—beginning with World War II—all of the lines on the chart swerved sharply upward. In the postwar period the lines in unison went vertical. Executives found the presentation interesting. But for the most part they then went back to business as usual. Few understood the implications of what they had heard.

It was around that time that Alvin Toffler's *Future Shock* burst upon the scene, to be followed in the 1980s by John Naisbitt's *Megatrends*. Futurist Naisbitt concluded, "We are living in the *time of the parenthesis, the time between eras*. It is as though we have bracketed off the present from both the past and the future, for we are neither here nor there. . . . We have done the human thing; we are clinging to the known past in fear of the unknown future."[5]

Hammer and Champy make this observation: "We already know that customers and competition have changed, but so, too, has the nature of change itself. Foremost, change has become both pervasive and persistent. It *is* normality." And a further caution from the authors of *Reengineering the Corporation*: "The changes that will put a company out of business are those that happen outside the light of its current expectations, and that is the source of most change in today's business environment."[6]

In a bewilderingly uncertain, fast-changing world, what is the leader of an organization to do? Just as meteorologists take little comfort in seeing sunny, blue skies directly overhead and instead scan their Nexrad and Doppler radars for the telltale blips of the next impending storm, organizations should be sweeping their skies with the radar of customer satisfaction measurement.

The weather metaphor is apropos. When it comes to understanding customers, most companies are like the old timer in the town square who believes it is going to rain when his arthritis kicks up. His weather instrument is the *Old Farmer's Almanac,* and he puts his faith in folklore: red sky at night, sailor's delight; red sky in morning, sailor take warning.

Just as today's instruments of meteorology are better at predicting rain than arthritis is, the Nexrad radar of customer satisfaction is a fully operational system of organizational telemetry that picks up on change and signals the need for decision making and action. It is an essential ingredient in reengineering. Unfortunately, many companies that have become enthralled with the concept of reengineering have simply reengineered systems that shouldn't exist at all, or have made wonderful improvements in productivity surrounding products or services that the market no longer wants, or soon won't.

If reengineering means starting with a clean slate, one of the first things that needs to be written on the slate is an accurate description of customer expectations, now and into the future insofar as they can be demystified. To start with anything else is folly.

To be effective, reengineerers need to understand the atmospherics of their environment, both outside and inside their organization. Here the issue is compounded. Reengineering requires cultural change. Becoming customer-centered requires cultural change. Organizations that attempt either or both of these initiatives without addressing the cultural change imperative are doomed to frustrating and expensive failure.

*Reengineering the Corporation* paints a gloomy picture:

> The cultural values found in some traditional companies are the byproducts of fragmented management systems which focus on past performance, emphasize control, and enshrine the hierarchy. Whatever such a company's value statement might *say*, its management systems may in fact promote values something like this:
>
> - My boss pays my salary; for all the talk about serving customers, the real objective is to keep the boss happy.
> - I'm just a cog in the wheel; my best strategy is to keep my head down and not make waves.
> - The more direct reports I have, the more important I am. The one with the biggest empire wins.
> - Tomorrow will be just like today; it always has been.[7]

Hammer and Champy contend that the *primary shapers* of employees' values and beliefs are an organization's management systems, including performance evaluation, compensation, recognition, and promotion through the ranks. That may be true in traditional organizations, but it will not be so in the customer-centered organizations of the future.

When organizational telemetry is in place, measuring every twitch and raised eyebrow of customers, both external and internal, and of the measurement system becomes a key part of the cultural primacy in the organization. Then values and beliefs rest on bedrock. In many sports, the number one imperative is to watch the ball; in business, it is to watch the customer.

This point was not lost on Raymond L. Manganelli and Mark M. Klein when they wrote the *Reengineering Handbook.* After describing the first step in a reengineering effort—getting prepared—they move on to the second step: a task they call modeling customers. "It is entirely appropriate," they write, "that business process reengineering start with the customer, because all of the things that a company wants—profits, prestige, the psychic rewards of success—ultimately stem from the customer. These are the payoff from playing the game called business. On the other hand, the price of being a player in the game is to meet the needs of the customer fairly completely and fairly consistently. Today's competitive environment provides few niches in which a company can survive if it doesn't adequately serve its customers."[8]

Manganelli and Klein also address an issue that has brought derision upon the reengineering efforts of many companies. Observers are critical of reengineering as a smoke screen for downsizing and wholesale layoffs. In the *Reengineering Handbook,* the authors make this point: "Although the primary focus of a reengineering project may be, say, cost reduction, customer satisfaction is a moving target. While your company is busy reducing costs, chances are the competition is improving customer service."[9]

Customer modeling is defined as gaining a complete understanding of the customers, their relationship to the organization, and, most important, their expectations. At this point, the authors of the handbook cop a plea. "Customer service and customer satisfaction," they write, "are the subjects of an extensive body of literature in their own right, which we will not attempt to reproduce."[10] They do suggest that information available in the company should be carefully validated by the reengineering team; when the understanding of the customer is inadequate, reengineering teams should consider customer interviews, customer surveys, and inviting key customers to participate in the reengineering project.

They advise reengineering teams to be careful to distinguish between what a customer says and what the customer means. And they caution teams to know who the customer really is, noting the distinction between resellers and ultimate users.

Instead of imploring a reengineering team to start by modeling the customer, perhaps a better approach is to assign a team to assess the company's existing channels of customer satisfaction measurement and design an effective system of organizational telemetry. Once that is accomplished, the groundwork has been laid for deciding what reengineering tasks to undertake and the priorities to be assigned.

If systems for understanding customers are lacking or inadequate, reengineering efforts are likely to get off to a shaky start. Having been instructed to model customers, the team heads off in that direction. But it is not a simple task, because meanwhile there is probably management pressure to get on with preconceived reengineering targets such as streamlining some administrative process.

There are enough problems in getting teams to function effectively, as described in another chapter of this book, without starting them off with confused directions. The logical way and sequence to proceed with reengineering is this:

- Assess methods currently in place for listening to the voice of the customer.
- Identify and correct gaps and weaknesses in the present methods.
- Augment existing methods to complete a closed-loop model of organizational telemetry.
- Utilize the data, information, and knowledge derived from organizational telemetry to pinpoint critical customer satisfaction issues to be addressed by a reengineering team.
- After reengineering has been accomplished, measure its effectiveness on the gauges of customer satisfaction telemetry.
- Adjust processes on a continuing basis.

Hammer says reengineering "is the radical redesign of a company's business process, reinventing the way the business operates in order to meet the demands of a modern economy. It is about rethinking work, not eliminating jobs, and it does indeed succeed, as demonstrated at companies as diverse as AT&T, American Express, Sun Life Assurance, Ford, and Procter & Gamble."[11]

The success of reengineering as a buzzword is demonstrated by the verbal fireworks it engenders among business gurus. Gary Hamel and C. K. Prahalad snort that reengineering "has more to do with shoring up today's businesses than creating tomorrow's industries."[12] Hammer fires back, "[T]hey are wrong. Reengineering has everything to do with creating and cultivating innovative strategies. By significantly improving a firm's operating capabilities, the technique allows it to implement new strategies and, even more importantly, leads it to envision entirely new strategic options."[13]

# References

1. Michael Hammer and James Champy, *Reengineering the Corporation* (New York: HarperCollins, 1993), p. 17.
2. Ibid., p. 18.
3. Ibid., p. 18.
4. Ibid.
5. John Naisbitt, *Megatrends* (New York: Warner Books, 1982).

6. Hammer and Champy, *Reengineering the Corporation*, pp. 23, 24.
7. Ibid., pp. 75, 76.
8. Raymond L. Manganelli and Mark M. Klein, *Reengineering Handbook* (New York: AMACOM), pp. 77, 80.
9. Ibid.
10. Ibid.
11. "Management Focus: Hammer Defends Reengineering," *The Economist* (November 5, 1994), p. 70.
12. Gary Hamel and C. K. Prahalad, *Competing for the Future* (Boston: Harvard Business School Press, 1994).
13. "Management Focus," *The Economist*.

# 10

# Learning Organization

Peter Senge's remarkable book *The Fifth Discipline: The Art and Practice of the Learning Organization,* has been described, perhaps unfairly, by some businesspeople as the most purchased and least read business book of our time.

Despite the fact that many say they found it tough going, the book nonetheless has had a profound impact. It is not uncommon now to hear even the crustiest traditional managers talk about learning, not just training.

It has become the conventional wisdom that the ability of people in organizations to learn is perhaps the only remaining area where lasting competitive advantage can be achieved. Gone are the days when size, wealth, and power provided an insurmountable bastion. Technology is readily available to even the smallest companies. The same is true of information, and, to some degree, capital. The L word is about all that is left.

## Traditional Hierarchies Don't Support Learning

In discussion of learning, traditional management comes in for its usual ration of abuse. Senge writes, "It is abundantly clear that rigid authoritarian hierarchies thwart learning, failing both to harness the spirit, enthusiasm, and knowledge of people throughout the organization and to be responsive to shifting business conditions."[1]

Not surprisingly, Senge sees the alternative as the learning organization, which he describes in this way: "While traditional organizations require management systems that control people's behavior, learning organizations invest in improving the quality of thinking, the capacity for reflection and team learning, and the ability to develop shared visions and shared understandings of complex business issues."

One of the people Senge likes to quote is Bill O'Brien, president of Hanover Insurance, who says, "Our traditional hierarchical organizations are not designed to provide for people's higher order needs, self-respect and self-actualization. The ferment in management will continue until organizations begin to address these needs, for all employees."[2]

What Senge and O'Brien say—ideas echoed by numerous opinion leaders—represents a tall order in organizations spinning their wheels in traditional ruts. In such organizations, training often amounts to a group of people seated classroom style, bored into somnolence by the droning of a dull instructor.

This McGuffey Reader-era approach to education is, sadly, still practiced in both schools and business. It is about as far removed from Senge's learning organization ideas as the stick drawings of kindergartners are from the masterworks in the Louvre.

A rethinking of what training and learning are all about is occurring as a result of very practical business considerations. Peter Kline and Bernard Saunders, in *Ten Steps to a Learning Organization*, explain: "Many organizations find themselves dependent on the wise decision making of a high percentage of their workers, since operations are far too complex to be understood by a small group of managers. Thus human freedom and responsibility is actually increased by technology. This development points to the need for a significant new style of management."[3]

In other words, everyone together is smarter than anyone alone.

## Effective Adult Learning

Companies are being compelled to consider the issue of what works and what doesn't in the field of adult learning. Most of the managers wrestling with the issue do so in the context of their own educational experience in high school and college. In many cases, those experiences were less than uplifting.

Recent research into adult learning has established interesting characteristics that human resource people and training directors would do well to consider. The most effective model seems to be self-directed learning, as opposed to the old idea of sitting at the knee of a master.[4] It seems that when people learn through their own initiative, they usually learn more effectively and retain what they learn longer than what is imposed on them by others. Adult learners share important characteristics:

- They have a deep need to be self-directing, but they have to be helped to overcome their conditioning from previous experience that students are dependent on teachers.
- They usually bring into any learning situation previous experience and training that provide a rich resource for helping each other learn.
- They tend to be task-centered, problem-centered, and life-centered (rather than subject-centered) in their orientation to learning.
- Primarily, they are intrinsically (rather than extrinsically) motivated to learn, given the right conditions and support.

# The Role of Customer Satisfaction in the Learning Organization

What, you may be thinking, does this have to do with customer satisfaction? A great deal. To address first the adult learning perspective, customer satisfaction plays a key role in the learning organization concept.

## Self-Directed

For people to sustain self-directed motivation to learn and grow, it has to make sense to them. There has to be a purpose. To supplant dependence on a teacher or a boss, people need goals they can identify with. Together, a commitment to serve internal and external customers and measurement that shows how well that goal is being met can provide the impetus for continuous learning.

Just as learning is a lifetime pursuit, as opposed to a task with a beginning and end, so too is responding to the everchanging expectations of customers. When the two become linked in the minds of employees, the seeds have been sown for the self-direction that adult learners thrive on.

## Life Experiences

Everyone has experience in being a customer. In an environment where that experience is recognized and respected, people are comfortable in sharing ideas and supporting each other's learning and development.

How different such an environment is from the sterile classroom setting: people meet for the purpose of figuring out how better to serve customers, and then they seek the information and knowledge they need to accomplish improvement tasks that they set for themselves.

## Task-Centered

If there is an understood purpose for learning something—how to solve a problem or perform a task—the adult learner grasps information more quickly and retains it better than when information is presented academically for its own sake.

The many tasks and specifics that grow out of a continuous improvement effort aimed at heightening customer satisfaction provide the kind of study checklist that adult learners respond to best.

## Intrinsic Motivation

The case can be made that the only sustainable motivation comes from within: self-motivation, doing things because (for whatever reason) you want to do them. Employees who draw their satisfaction from serving customers, and from growing in their ability to do so, receive constant stimulation and support. When it is clear that a self-directed program of continuous learning enhances their job satisfaction and sense of fulfillment in their work, employees approach learning with enthusiasm. Motivation is no longer an issue.

Executives confronted with the need to make decisions about how to spend training dollars have more issues to grapple with than the specifics of adult learning. There is also the gnarly issue of the generation gap. Actually it is gaps plural. Top management people, many of whom are in their fifties, puzzle over the attitudes of the Baby Busters who are following them up the corporate ladder. And the Busters can't for the life of them understand the Generation Xers who are toiling under them.

This is not a new phenomenon, of course. The ancient Greeks despaired about what would happen when the unruly young took over. It has been ever thus. The issue stands out in especially bold relief now because the accelerated pace of change draws more extreme lines. The evidence shows up glaringly in today's workplace.

The inclination of today's young people to challenge the way things are done may seem like impertinence to older executives who grew up thinking that you should keep quiet until you are handed the key to the executive washroom. There is agreement among the experts that Generation X workers are less motivated by financial concerns than their predecessors. They are less interested in committing themselves body and soul to the job in return for a Beemer and a Gold Card. There is more to life than a job, they shrug.

However, generation Xers *can* identify with customer satisfaction. It resonates with their desire to understand the business at its core. It appeals to their altruism and genuine feelings about being of service to their fellow humans. The people-centered basics of customer satisfaction are an antidote to the rampant materialism that the young are challenging.

Many observers feel that today's young workers are a broadly well-informed group. They see more of what the world has to offer, and they make decisions according to that. They are credited with moving more quickly. They will not put up with failures in communication; they want to be informed, in both the short and the long term.

Xers have grown up accepting corporate instability. Unlike their predecessors, they haven't been sold the myth of job security. It is not a part of their reality or consciousness. Not only are they willing to accept the truth, but they won't settle for less than honesty.

There is no question about customer satisfaction, not job security, being the driving force in the Davanni's Pizza and Hot Hoagies chain. Chris Preefe, manager of a Davanni's store in St. Paul, Minnesota, has a workforce of mostly eighteen- to twenty-five-year-olds. "One thing [management] people often forget to do is ask their [employees'] opinions," he says. "It's a good idea to get the employees involved in making decisions—making things faster, better, smarter. More times than not, their ideas are better than ours, especially when it involves the day-to-day things like preparing and serving food—things we as managers don't do on a regular basis."[5]

The essence is respect for the individual—whether that's the worker whose ideas can make a difference, or the customer whose satisfaction is at the heart of business success. It's a tough lesson to learn for people whose thoughts run more to market share points, economic value added, and head counts.

Symbiosis occurs in organizations committed to learning and being customer-centered. To keep up with the mercurial customer requires the ability to learn new things and new ways—continuously. This enforced learning stimulates and enriches the lives of employees and executives alike.

# References

1. Peter Senge, *The Fifth Discipline: The Art and Practice of the Learning Organization* (New York: Doubleday, 1990), p. 289.
2. Ibid., p. 140.
3. Peter Kline and Bernard Saunders, *Ten Steps to a Learning Organization* (Arlington, Va.: Great Ocean Publishers, 1993), p. 13.
4. Robert M. Smith, *Learning to Learn Across the Lifespan* (San Francisco: Jossey-Bass, 1990).
5. Dan Emerson, "Today's Workforce Needs More," *City Business* (June 30, 1995), p. 11.

# 11

# Teams

In the panoply of new management ideas for the new age, the one most misunderstood and most frequently goofed up is probably the concept of teams. In any case, lively argument on the subject of teams is assured.

Teams are important to the subject of customer satisfaction simply because in the most progressive organizations work, both day-to-day and in regard to continuous improvement, is accomplished through teams. If customer satisfaction is regarded as a pervasive driving force, it necessarily seeps into the charter and mission of every team.

There are parallels between the concept of teams as an effective organizational technique and total quality management. Only a hard-bitten iconoclast could find fault with either idea. Yet the organizational landscape is littered with failed programs in both areas that started out with the best of intentions.

In *The Wisdom of Teams,* Jon R. Katzenbach and Douglas K. Smith make the case for teams: "We believe that teams—real teams, not just groups that management calls 'teams'—should be the basic unit of performance for most organizations, regardless of size. In any situation requiring the real-time combination of multiple skills, experiences, and judgments, a team inevitably gets better results than a collection of individuals operating within confined job roles and responsibilities. Teams are more flexible than larger organizational groupings because they can be more quickly assembled, deployed, refocused, and disbanded, usually in ways that enhance rather than disrupt more permanent structures and processes. Teams are more productive than groups that have no clear performance objectives because their members are committed to deliver tangible performance results. Teams and performance are an unbeatable combination."[1]

# Why Teams Fail

So what is the problem? The first thought expressed in the quotation above: the distinction between real teams and groups that management calls teams. Simply bringing a group of people together and calling them a team does not make a team.

## Purpose

First, is it clear what kind of team is being formed? Is it a team to make recommendations about a specific issue (often called a task force)? Or is it a team with the purpose of making or doing things? Or a team for the purpose of running things (a management team)? Confusion about the purpose of a team almost guarantees its ineffectiveness.

## Assignment

After the right combination of people is assembled and they are given a clear definition of what kind of team they are to be, the next issue is the nature of their assignment. What precisely are they supposed to do? Teams that get fuzzy direction in this regard often have a very hard time producing results.

Executives who resort to teams as a substitute for making decisions themselves—the kind of decisions *they* should be making—often aren't clear themselves on what they want the team to do. They maintain a wait-and-see attitude and reserve the right to approve or disapprove what the team does. This, too, is a formula for team failure.

Then there are the executives who are suddenly overcome with warm egalitarianism. They see the team members as empowered equals who need to figure out for themselves what they should be doing. They don't think it is right to be specific on their expectations for the team. They believe it punctures the balloon of empowerment.

There is an appropriate middle ground between the extremes of overdirecting and underdirecting teams. At the very least, the team needs to know what the end product of its work should be: a new process, a new product, a solution to a problem, a report, a plan. It needs to know its level of authority: whether it can act, and if not, what approval process is required. It needs to know what resources are available to accomplish its work, and the general time frame in which it is expected to function.

# People

Katzenbach and Smith talk about combining skills, knowledge, and experience on what are usually referred to as cross-functional teams. Selecting the right people to be on a team is an art requiring the utmost skill and sensitivity. Just as an experienced host knows that the success of a party depends on inviting the right combination of people, careful selection of team members can foreordain the outcome.

## Team Leadership

There are a number of key issues that revolve around the leadership of teams. To many people, the very idea of leadership in a team environment is contradictory. The various definitions of *team* usually include some reference to mutual accountability. If team members are instructed to conduct themselves as equals governed by mutual accountability, the objection goes, how can there be a leader?

There is so much baggage associated with the idea of a leader that it is sometimes difficult to get people to understand that teams still have leadership functions needing to be carried out. These functions can be shared and rotated under some circumstances so there is a kind of virtual leader. Or the team can choose a leader from among its members. Or a leader can be appointed at the outset. The process for choosing a leader is not nearly as important as the fact that there must be a leader.

Some of the necessary leadership functions are:

- Keeping the vision focused
- Scheduling meetings and setting meeting agendas
- Facilitating meetings
- Administrative discipline: making sure reports get done, budgets prepared and submitted
- Making sure team members get recognition and encouragement
- Conflict resolution
- Communications

The idea of leadership on a team should not be confused with the stereotypical idea of a boss. Teams do not need, nor should they have, bosses. They do need certain functions performed that fall within the definition of leadership. Juries need foremen, and committees need chairpersons. How the leadership is chosen is irrelevant; the fact that leadership must exist is not.

There is an old saw—what is everybody's job is nobody's job—to which teams risk falling victim. The concept of mutual accountability, often in the form of peer pressure, plays an important role, especially under the subtle direction of a skilled leader. But there is no substitute for the individual, acknowledged leader.

Katzenbach and Smith talk about "tangible performance results." That, of course, is what management expects when it creates teams. But it is not always what ensues. To whom should management turn when teams flounder? The answer, of course, is the leader. How do you hold a leaderless team accountable?

Customer satisfaction can and should play a crucial role in supporting the leaders of teams. The customer can become their badge of authority. If the vision is to serve the customer, and team leaders position themselves as representing the interests of customers, they don't need corporate titles to be effective.

## Motivating Team Members

The boss taps you on the shoulder and says, "I want you to be on this team." Think for a moment about the questions that run through your mind:

- How am I going to get my job done if I have to spend a lot of time in meetings?
- How am I going to fit in with these people I don't know?
- Am I going to get paid for the extra work involved?
- Is the work of the team going to be important, or is it just an exercise?
- Who is going to be in charge?
- Am I going to have two bosses now?
- How long is this going to go on?
- How is this going to affect my career?
- How important is this to management?
- Why did they pick me?
- What kind of work is involved?

Until these questions are answered satisfactorily, people are likely to sit in meetings with their arms crossed and their minds closed. If there is no shared vision in the organization, and the old style of management is alive and well, people appointed to teams spend more time thinking about the pecking order than about dealing with the issue at hand.

By contrast, what if everyone in an organization knows full well that the driving force of the organization is customer satisfaction? Individuals are recognized and rewarded for going to extremes to serve customers (both internal and external). Leaders of the organization live the vision of customer satisfaction daily.

In this kind of organization, people appointed to teams don't even think about the questions mentioned above. They know that the only possible reason for a team is to advance the cause of customer satisfaction in some way. They know that they will benefit personally in direct proportion to their contribution in behalf of customers. They know that their leaders and fellow workers are motivated by the same vision.

The team is equipped to make fact-based decisions, grounded in the reality of the information flowing into the company through customer satisfaction measurement. Whether the issue is primarily an internal one (developing more efficient processes), or external (creating a new product or service), there is data to get the job started.

Starting with data—incontrovertible facts derived through organizational telemetry—obviates the kind of discussion that causes teams to bog down early in their work. When people revert to expressing their opinions, founded or unfounded, there is no substitute for facts as a way to get the process moving along again.

## Cultural Change Must Precede the Teams

Many organizations have attempted to transplant the team idea into their culture like a surgeon transplanting an organ. The transplanting of organs requires antirejection drugs. Unless organizations undertake cultural change, the grafting on of teams will result in rejection, with varying degrees of severity.

Wise leaders recognize that the traditional, hierarchical style of management is antithetical to teams. Remarkably, there are organizations with hundreds of teams in operation that have yet to discover this truth. They keep tinkering with the team idea, trying to make it work, without facing the reality that their culture must change—perhaps drastically.

Obviously, it is not a new idea that the rigid, hidebound organizational structures of the past must change, if for no other reason than sheer survival. The problem, the dilemma, the enigma is: Change to what? Teams are one among the many ideas summoned to fill that gap. Some of the ideas grasped by executives unsure of themselves miss their potential by being adopted in the wrong sequence. Teams are a case in point. Katzenbach and Smith contend that "the dynamics that drive teams mirror the behaviors and values necessary to the high-performance organization."[2]

A mirror cannot reflect something that doesn't exist. Behaviors and values are elements of an organizational culture. Therefore (with the exception of some unusually advanced organizations) cultural change must precede the creation of teams if they are to make a contribution to achieving the attributes of a high-performance organization. Many organizations put the cart before the horse and wonder why the rig doesn't move out smartly.

## Executives and the Team Concept

Another common problem is that executives who jump on the team bandwagon don't understand the nuances of teams because they have never been on one themselves. The team idea is new enough that there are many senior executives who moved into leadership positions before teams came into use in their companies. Executives who got ahead because they were recognized as having "command presence," and who settled easily into positions adorned by power and influence, haven't experienced the give-and-take of a team environment, where no one is permitted to call the shots. To these executives, the process seems simple enough: Get the right people together, put them in a room, tell them what the problem is, and let them solve it. No big deal; let's get on with it. It is a rare executive who can truly understand the team experience without having been through it.

Hard-driving executives, unschooled in the functioning of teams, often have little patience for the subject of corporate culture. As one old-timer was heard to remark when he heard about a conference on corporate culture, "In my day, we didn't have any of that culture stuff."

Stripped of psychosocial jargon, corporate culture is simply "the way we do things around here." The way things are done can work either for or against the team idea. The way things are done is often the biggest obstacle in the path of becoming a high-performance organization.

Although many executives haven't served on teams as the term is understood in today's business environment, being in top management tends to be a team job itself. Peter Drucker made the point: "Whatever the titles on the organization chart, the top-management job in a healthy company is almost always actually done by a team." But Drucker adds this caution: "Just because the organization chart shows a top-management team does not necessarily mean that there is one. There is a need for safeguards against the danger of dictatorships disguised as a top-management team."[3]

# When Is a Team Not a Team?

Equally, there is a need for safeguards against traditional organizational structures disguised as a team approach.

The concept of leading an enterprise that does its creative work through teams has excited many people. But it has also deteriorated into something very narrow and ineffective. Peters and Waterman commented on this phenomenon in *In Search of Excellence*. After heaping praise on the idea of the ad hoc task force, they hastened to add, "Unfortunately, it can also become the quintessence of hopeless bureaucracy." They reported that in many companies task forces became just one additional part of the rigid system they were meant to fix: "Task forces became nothing more than coordinating committees—with a different name. Like other management tools adopted in the wrong context, the task force made things worse, not better."[4]

What, then, is the context in which teams should be created and allowed to function? There is an exciting description of how it can be in a book called *The Inventive Organization,* by organizational development consultant Jill Janov. Here is her view of the right context:

> A wonderful metaphor for interdependence exists in the cocreationist theory of literature. This fancy term refers to a theory that until an author has written and a reader has read, there is no book. An author often intends for the reader to get certain meaning from his work that the reader does not get. And, conversely, the reader often reads into the work something the author did not intend. Thus neither creates the book. The book is created out of the interaction between the author and the reader and out of the individual experience of each.
>
> Organizations are created out of relationships—relationships between customers and suppliers, leaders and followers, and between individuals and the means by which they produce. These relationships cocreate the enterprise.

If we see our organizations existing in relationship to our customer requirements, we will see our "selves" existing in relationship to our customers. This relationship is one of interdependence. It can be one of partnership if we expand our concept of our organization—extend the boundary we have drawn around the organizational system so that the customer is included in our definition of the enterprise.[5]

It can be said that the organization that creates a team, the individuals who make up that team, and the customers who interact with the organization are all cocreationists. What they create through their interaction could not occur in any other way and is thus a product of the creation process.

# References

1. Jon R. Katzenbach and Douglas K. Smith, *The Wisdom of Teams* (New York: Harper Business, 1993).
2. Ibid., p. 250.
3. Peter Drucker, *Management Tasks, Responsibilities, Practices* (New York: Harper & Row, 1973), p. 618.
4. Tom Peters and Robert Waterman, *In Search of Excellence* (New York: Warner Books, 1982), p. 128.
5. Jill Janov, *The Inventive Organization* (San Francisco: Jossey-Bass, 1996), pp. 200–201.

# 12

# Leadership

With so many excellent books on leadership in business currently out, there is no need to repeat here the fundamentals of leadership. However, there is a yawning gap in the literature concerning the role of leadership as it relates to becoming a customer-centered organization.

A fundamental truth is often overlooked: It is difficult, if not impossible, for an organization to become genuinely customer-centered if the leadership is not fully and relentlessly committed to the idea and understands the role management must play to support it. Often, the issue is not what executives say but what they do—or don't do. Most executives realize they are being watched intently by their employees. But sometimes they fail to realize the signals they are emitting, especially as to how they feel about customers.

Consider for a moment some anomalies that are commonplace.

A high degree of customer dissatisfaction—surveys show in the range of 80 percent—has nothing to do with product; it has to do with service and the general area of business relationships. Yet in many companies management's attention, quality programs, and spending are directed only toward product. What does this tell employees about management's beliefs and grasp of the issues?

It may seem obvious that revenue comes from outside of companies and is provided by customers. Yet if you monitor the activities of many executives, you find that a very high percentage of their time is devoted to internal considerations: talking to each other about what's going on in the company, studying reports on performance of departments, attending meetings, exerting financial control, making plans based primarily on internal considerations. Where is the customer in all of this?

Everyone knows that management's levers of power are compensation, recognition, promotions, and, ultimately, providing or withdrawing employment. Because abiding self-interest causes employees to observe carefully, they, too, know how and why management uses those levers. The influences they see are often short-term financial considerations, custom, tradition, seniority, favoritism, greed, sycophancy—not performance against the goal of customer satisfaction.

Imagine for a moment that in going to work on a Monday morning you find yourself on stage, under the spotlights, and in front of an audience of employees. They are making judgments about you, just as a theatrical audience judges performers. Every gesture, every arched eyebrow, every movement is interpreted as a signal of what kind of person you are. The audience listens to what you say while at the same time factoring in what you do, your relationship with others on the stage, and the overall impression created by the attitude that you convey. Finally, they judge your character, integrity, and beliefs. From this point on, forever, you are viewed through the lens of that judgment.

An actor on the stage knows how the playwright intends the audience to interpret the character being portrayed. Every nuance of the performance is crafted to guide what the audience believes about the character. Actors make the story understandable and believable.

Business executives, whether they like it or not, are on stage a great deal of the time. If they want to be understood and believed, it is important for them to be conscious of the unspoken as well as the spoken messages they convey, and the motivations behind their actions. Their audiences are incredibly perceptive.

What, then, is the best way for executives to get employees to see things from the executive's perspective? Most executives have neither the talent nor the desire to become accomplished actors. Under the circumstances, their best recourse is to just be themselves. That being the case, it is important for executives to take a good, hard look at their values. In being themselves, do they set an example they want the organization to follow?

A couple of examples illustrate this point.

I was once an executive of a company faced with a potentially complicated and costly recall of a product we manufactured. It was implicated in accidental explosions that had killed or maimed a number of people over a period of time. The question on the table was whether we should publicly announce a product recall.

It was not a simple issue. Millions of these products had been sold. There was a real risk of creating a public panic. The logistics of locating and modifying or replacing these devices was nightmarish. There were technical doubts about the causes of the explosions. Depending on the various scenario being considered, the potential cost—in dollars and corporate reputation—could be astronomical.

We set a meeting to make a decision on the recall. Involved were executives from engineering, production, public relations, advertising, marketing, sales, finance, and legal. The senior executive heading the meeting started by saying, "There is one issue here that is off the table, and I don't even want to hear it mentioned. And that is what this is going to cost us. We are going to make a decision based only on what is the right thing to do."

That clear-cut statement of integrity, honesty, and courage set the tone of the meeting and resulted in a sound decision, which was to announce and conduct a recall. Not only did it put the company in an unassailable position that protected its reputation, it also profoundly influenced all of the people in that meeting and their outlook on issues of ethics and integrity for the future.

Contrast that with the familiar examples of executives who play the blame game when the company is not performing very well. They say it is Wall Street's fault that the company has been forced into short-term thinking and shortsighted decisions, such as wholesale downsizing. Here's an actual quote from a CEO: "Talk to the good CEOs, and they'll tell you their top priority is to manage for the long-term strength of the business and its various stakeholders. But the fact is they're being forced by an increasingly impatient investment market to manage for the instant gratification of the shareholder."

This is like blaming a thermometer for the temperature. Top executives who make woe-is-me statements about how hard it is to run a business these days, while at the same time banking multimillion-dollar salaries, shouldn't be surprised when their employees begin acting cynically.

There are many examples of self-defeating behavior at the executive level that erode even the best of intentions concerning customer satisfaction. One of the most damaging is an inordinate emphasis on profits—and I emphasize *inordinate*. It is important that my point not be misunderstood. Obviously, profit is very important. A business cannot exist for long without it. It is the fuel needed for getting better, and if you're not getting better you are getting worse, with a dismal outcome being only a matter of time.

Executives should remember, though, that profitability is an effect, not a cause. Management needs to be dealing with causes, just as doctors are more concerned about healing disease than treating symptoms. Constant harping on profit tends to obscure the sources of profit—the ultimate source, of course, being the decision of a customer to trade dollars for goods and services.

An emphasis on profits becomes inordinate when employees are led to believe it is the most important driving force in the business, when their perception is that management is single-mindedly devoted to profits to the exclusion of all else. The danger is that in most businesses it is relatively easy to drive up profits through decisions that lead to ultimate collapse. Does this mean management shouldn't pay attention to profits? Of course not. Does it mean that there is a need for a so-called balanced scorecard in the messages leaders convey about what is important? Absolutely.

Another self-defeating behavior is the one on which parents are often called to task: Do as I say, not as I do. Examples are leaders who talk about customer satisfaction but spend little time with customers, who make disparaging remarks about customers, who pay no attention to data on customer satisfaction, and who treat complaints as unwarranted intrusion.

The executive office can be a pleasant and serene place where cultural customs are understood and observed. There are built-in protections from the cacophony of the outside world. It is tempting for executives to stay in comfortable cocoons. By contrast, the customer world can be raucous, challenging, uncomfortable, disagreeable, unsettling, ungrateful. When leaders spend their time and energy on a long list of priorities considered more important than customer relationships—activities suited to the comforts of the executive office—any exhortations they make to employees to be customer-focused, -driven, or -centered are likely to be disregarded, or at least discounted.

The decision-making process in companies is revealing—and closely watched by employees. This is where the billowing clouds of rhetoric part, revealing hard reality. If management uses this opportunity to frame decisions in the context of what is best for the customer, a strongly reinforcing message goes out to the organization. The exact opposite happens if the customer is ignored.

Whether executives are aware of it or not—or for that matter whether they even care—employees are acutely sensitive to which values are being honored in the decision-making process. Is thinking short-term or long-term? Are employees supported in what they are asked to do? Is the voice of the customer heard? Is management saying the same things behind closed doors that it says in employee meetings?

Despite seminars, workshops, and books on the distinction between management and leadership, it is still not clear in the minds of many. Even executives who have thought about it deeply and want very much to be leaders still spend most of their time on management things. Still, there may be a simple distinction from the perspective of our discussion: It has been said that management is doing things right, while leadership is doing the right things.

Gandhi said, "There go my people. I must follow them, for I am their leader." The statement reveals a depth of wisdom, humility, and understanding of human nature that is not common in executive suites.

The leader of a customer-centered organization must first of all inspire and enable cultural change. This is perhaps the most challenging assignment anyone could have. It contrasts with issuing orders, making tough decisions, and maintaining organizational discipline—the usual management activities that are relatively straightforward compared to providing the vision and inspiration for revolutionary change.

Leadership involves the creation of an environment in which people do things because they believe in them and want to do them—not because they need the money, or fear losing their jobs, or are apprehensive about punishment. Leadership is present when people raise their own sights and perform better than they ever thought they could.

Leadership is present when people accept new ideas, convinced that they thought them up themselves, and refuse to settle for less than the best from themselves and their fellow workers. Leadership is calm, confident, positive, encouraging, gracious, and patient.

For a leader to hold up the vision of a customer-centered organization is a bold step, involving risk and commitment. It can be achieved only when leaders understand and accept the consequences, only with buy-in at all levels of the organization and consistent support at the top for the principles involved. The fact of the matter is, people's thoughts cannot be controlled. But they can be influenced.

It is not surprising that when customer satisfaction is discussed in these terms there are executives who reject the idea. Either they simply don't see it as anything that far-reaching, or they don't grasp the need for sweeping change in their organization, or they think a major initiative would be too disruptive. There may be an inner voice saying, "I didn't get here by making waves and taking risks; why would I want to do that now?"

Many executives simply haven't thought the issue through. "Customer satisfaction? It's a matter of taking some surveys and training people to be nicer. That's it, period; it's certainly not a strategic issue or anything that requires much of a budget. And besides, most of the customers are reasonably happy and keep coming back."

For leaders who have crossed these thresholds and are ready to think about more advanced issues, the next consideration must be the attitudes and morale of the people in the organization, from top to bottom. What are their beliefs? What are their mores? How is the culture influencing them to behave? What are the forces at work that mitigate against customer satisfaction?

In the supervisory tradition, people can't be trusted and need to be controlled. "They need rules and regulations. You have to keep your eye on them, or they'll goof off and steal you blind. For the most part, people are not very bright, and they are expendable." (Of course, the work environment today in many organizations has advanced beyond these blatant attitudes, but the undercurrents are still there.) Psychologists say the reality is quite to the contrary. Most people want to do a good job, but they need to feel that their work matters. They are committed when it is clear to them that they have responsibilities that contribute to the success of the company.

Just as people have very good waffle meters, they also have excellent irrelevance meters. They know when they are being asked to do things that aren't directly connected to the business of the organization. They know when their work can't be measured in terms of its impact on the business. They know when they are just going through the motions for paper-shuffling, bureaucratic reasons.

An important job for the leader of a customer-centered organization is to help people at all levels to understand how their responsibilities contribute to the organization's results. One way is to point out that the customer pays the bills, and therefore anything done to help satisfy customers contributes to the employee's paycheck. That's a start, but it really needs to be made more personal than that. The more clearly people see the importance of their individual contribution, the more significant they feel and the stronger their motivation to perform well.

When employees are given the opportunity to express themselves freely and openly, without fear of the consequences, they are likely to send these messages to their leaders:

- Don't assume we know what's going on, or that we think about things the same way you do. Communication in this organization needs a lot of work.
- You may think you know what I want to do with my career, but you are probably wrong. I have ideas, dreams, and ambitions that might surprise you.
- We look to management to set the boundaries. It helps when management makes clear what can and can't be done.

- It helps a lot to have a well-defined vision for the organization. That's management's job, but we'd like to be involved in the process.
- You expect us to live the vision, but don't forget we expect that of you, too.

This is so different from the us-against-them mentality that exists in many organizations— *us* being the anointed few in the executive suite, and *them* being the proletariat masses, otherwise known as workers, employees, nonexempts, or some other class distinction. It is imperative in the creation of a customer-centered organization that the class-distinction mindset, wherever it exists, be dissolved. It will only happen through the exercise of strong leadership.

# Part Three

# IMPACT ON FUNCTIONAL UNITS

**W**hile many organizations profess to have the customer uppermost in their thoughts, the reality of life in their organization testifies to the contrary. Examining the daily activities, department by department, function by function, reveals a range of imperatives that have little or nothing to do with the relationship to customers.

The following chapters cover in detail how customer-centeredness can influence the way key departments function. It contrasts enlightened, customer-driven attitudes and activities with the traditional way of doing business and lays out a conceptual framework for each department or functional area of an organization to pursue in recognizing the customer as CEO.

# 13

# Your People

Trying to get an organization of people who are unhappy in their work to satisfy customers is like trying to form an orchestra with people who don't want to play their instruments. It can't be done. Yet strangely enough, that is what executives of many organizations attempt to do. You hear it all the time: pronouncements about satisfying (and more hyperbolically *delighting*) customers, made to workforces that are demoralized, disheartened, frightened, cynical, disillusioned, and bitter.

If Murphy's Law were updated, one more could be added to this effect: "The more executives that use hyperbole to describe how they satisfy customers, the less likely their company is to have good, solid programs to build customer satisfaction."

A top priority for organizations that are serious about customer satisfaction must be to attend to the attitudes and feelings of their own people—a complex subject if there ever was one in this age of transformation. Once customer satisfaction measurement is fully understood and effectively utilized, it can become the focal point of a vision that energizes an organization from top to bottom. On the other hand, if customer satisfaction is just another empty slogan, it serves only to deepen the cynicism and bitterness that erode morale.

A middle manager at a Fortune 500 company once shared with me an experience that illustrates the point. The CEO of this company was a "we're gonna delight our customers" guy. This manager was excited about the idea; in fact, he developed a whole plan for his department that supported the customer focus and he was very proud of it.

One day his boss walked in. He saw an outline of the plan on the manager's white board and studied it quizzically. The manager was expecting to be complimented, but the boss said with a frown, "I want this crap erased. You know what your job is. Cut your costs and do it now. We don't have time for this namby pamby stuff." The manager told me he felt like he had been kicked in the stomach.

There is a lot to be learned from this sad little tale. Management by slogan doesn't work. In order to get buy-in at all levels of an organization, a vision has to be not only announced but explained and supported by policies and procedures. Until there is alignment of goals, objectives, and personal aspirations, there is only noise.

It is not uncommon for organizations to unwittingly mislead their people. They claim the mantle of customer satisfaction but reward the managers who achieve short-term profits regardless of the cost to customers. They proclaim that their employees are assets, but then treat them like liabilities. The CEO talks about the importance of customers but hobnobs mostly with other CEOs and top executives.

Extraordinarily successful organizations have been compared to cults. Cults usually are based on simple ideas that resonate among their members at a primal level (believe in the idea and in the charismatic leader who expresses it, and all of your problems are solved). The early and enormously successful IBM was cultlike. Wal-Mart today is a customer satisfaction cult in the best sense of the word. People want to have something to believe in, a vision to share. Contrary to the basis for a lot of management thinking in the past fifty years, most people want to do a good job. They want their work to matter. They want to make a contribution. They want to feel valued. They want to be listened to. If all of these conditions apply, they work their hearts out.

Is that so hard to grasp?

There is a rallying point that everyone can understand and support: the customer. Some companies have tried stressing that the customer is paying the bills, including wages. However, there is a more positive thought that appeals at the most basic of human levels. Organizations, and everyone in them, have as their purpose *serving* the customer. A commitment to serving customers feels good and is intellectually honest. It has a firmer moral base than serving oneself. It is more justifiable than serving management, or fellow workers, or stockholders, or creditors, or Wall Street, or any amorphous community. Furthermore, if customers are well served, other constituencies benefit proportionately. There are no losers.

When executives begin thinking about customer satisfaction, there is frequently a knee-jerk reaction: "Let's get some customer service training. Let's teach our people how to be nice to customers." It is often referred to derisively as "smile training." If employees are basically dissatisfied and disillusioned, the best you will get from smile training is forced and phony smiles that customers read clearly and react to negatively ("Have a nice day, my butt!").

Attempting to achieve customer satisfaction by spending a few bucks on customer service training is comparable to trying to achieve quality by putting up some posters and teaching the machinists statistical process control. It is a hot coal of inspiration tossed into a sea of indifference. It should be obvious, but apparently isn't, that if a company wants to be truly customer-centered it must have a workforce with high morale and a visceral commitment to serving. At the same time, customers dissatisfied with products, services, and policies can soon wipe the smiles off the most committed of employees.

Is this a catch-22? Seems you can't have customer satisfaction without satisfied employees, but you can't have satisfied employees without customer satisfaction. The answer lies in addressing both issues at the same time, helping all employees with a clear understanding of the strategy and plans to support it.

The importance of employee satisfaction was recognized by the designers of the Malcolm Baldrige National Quality Award. In the category of human resource development and management, there is a section on employee well-being and satisfaction. Contenders for the award are asked to describe how their company "maintains a work environment and a work climate conducive to the well-being and development of employees."

The award criteria include examples of factors that might affect satisfaction, well-being, and motivation:

> Effective employee problem or grievance resolution
> Safety
> Employee views of leadership and management
> Employee development and career opportunities
> Employee preparation for changes in technology or work
>     organization
> Work environment
> Workload
> Cooperation and teamwork
> Recognition
> Benefits
> Communications
> Job security
> Compensation
> Equality of opportunity
> Capability to provide required services to customers

To score well on the Baldrige, companies must have well-documented processes, systems, and procedures. The examiners are not taken in by applications (no matter how well written) that are not supported by evidence of effective activity. In the case of employee well-being and satisfaction, Baldrige examiners are trained to ask for documentation of how the company determines employee satisfaction, well-being, and motivation. They ask to see descriptions of methods; frequency of methods such as surveys; the specific factors used in this determination; and how the information is used to improve satisfaction, well-being, and motivation.

It is clear that the eminent authorities from many industries who contributed to the development of the Baldrige criteria saw clearly the relationship between employees' feelings about their work and the ability of companies to achieve quality as determined by customer satisfaction.

In a study of its customer-service centers, MCI found clear relationships between how employees felt about the quality of MCI services and their own job satisfaction. MCI also found a linkage between employee satisfaction and customer satisfaction.[1] Other studies have shown that employee turnover has a significant, adverse effect on customer satisfaction, which in turn impacts customer retention. Profit and growth are stimulated primarily by customer loyalty. Loyalty is a direct result of customer satisfaction. Satisfaction is largely influenced by the value of services provided to customers. Value is created by satisfied, loyal, and productive employees. Employee satisfaction, in turn, results primarily from high-quality support services and policies that enable employees to deliver results to customers.

Focusing on employee satisfaction, MCI probed to find out their employees' point of view. The factors they uncovered, in order of importance, were:

- Satisfaction with the job itself
- Training
- Pay
- Fairness in advancement
- Treatment with respect and dignity
- Teamwork
- The company's interest in the employee's well-being[2]

A good starting point is to find out how employees feel they are being treated with regard to the factors identified by MCI. This can be done best through a confidential survey that protects the anonymity of the respondents. When surveys are taken, it is crucial that summaries of the results be reported back to the employees, along with information on steps that will be taken to make improvements. Studies have shown that when survey results are not reported back and management fails to act on survey results, morale sinks lower than it was before the survey was taken. Simply stated, companies are better off not asking their employees questions unless they are willing to do something about the answers they get.

Customer Inc. in Minneapolis developed two questionnaires to find out how the client's employees feel about customer satisfaction. One is a seventeen-question mail survey intended for all employees of a company. The second is a twenty-four-question discussion outline for use in interviews with frontline employees who work daily with customers. (The two questionnaires are reproduced in Appendixes C and D respectively.)

In addition to morale-related questions, it is important to ask how employees think the organization could do a better job of responding to customer needs. People working directly with customers are a wellspring of information and ideas about improving customer relationships. An employee who advanced a brilliant solution for a tough problem that had vexed a company for years was asked why he hadn't come forward with his idea sooner. His answer was, "Nobody ever asked me before." That's an all-too-common waste of the know-how and intelligence of employees. A companion problem is the equally prevalent situation in which employee ideas and suggestions are ignored by insensitive and insecure managers who believe the only ideas of any value are the ones they come up with themselves.

An assessment of how employees feel about their jobs and how customer-centered they feel the organization is identifies specific areas needing attention. The best solution, however, is not to undertake a patchwork of fixes. Instead, create a pact, with the commitment of all employees from the CEO to the loading dock worker.

There are essentially two elements to the pact. First, the organization decides to become genuinely customer-centered, treating the customer as CEO. This commitment is thereafter the litmus test for all decision making. Employees are not expected to accept this on faith; it is proven by management action. Second, management understands that it is not possible to serve customers well and creatively unless employees feel they have a fair work environment in which they can grow and be fulfilled, and in which enthusiasm is genuine. Such an environment can be achieved only with mutual trust and understanding.

Unless there is an exceptional level of trust already established in an organization, the idea of such a two-pronged pact will be greeted by cool skepticism. An executive who gives a speech along these lines to an employee group is likely to experience stony silence. That's okay. It takes time and a lot of show-me activity to convince change-hardened employees that this time something really is different.

The following are ideas that have been used successfully by companies to demonstrate to employees that they mean what they say:

- Apply for the Baldrige Award. It is an obstacle course that a Marine drill sergeant would respect, a no-nonsense test of seriousness of intent. Nobody who carries out an honest application process ends up complacent or self-satisfied.
- Establish an active employee suggestion system, with recognition and rewards. Like a marriage, a suggestion system requires continuous injections of energy to keep it alive and thriving.
- Hold roundtable meetings: informal luncheons between management and small groups of line employees for genuine dialogue about complaints, concerns, and new ideas.
- Survey customers and employees; track and post results for all to see, making clear that the intent is to support management by fact.
- Make a commitment in dollars, on the order of 5 percent of sales, to provide training for workers in such areas as management, communications, systems, team effectiveness, and conflict resolution. Avoid the common mistake of allocating the majority of training dollars to management.
- Form partnerships with key suppliers and customers to gain access to their resources, ideas, and talents.
- Make it *impossible* to be out of touch with customers. For example, give customers personal pager numbers they can use to reach your customer contact personnel—even the CEO! Follow up by asking customers to rate their contacts on customer service, as well as quality, delivery, and communication.
- In each work area, set up bulletin boards where employees can post work-related problems that need resolution. Hold communication-board meetings wherein supervisors assign team members to problems. In plain view, post the problem and the name of the person responsible for solving it.

In a survey of 266 major North American companies, the international management consulting firm Towers Perrin found that the two activities believed most effective in supporting quality and customer service were employee involvement and training. The respondents overwhelmingly agree that more is needed than just the right attitude. Management needs to provide training in skills, knowledge, and competencies if their companies are to do a better job of satisfying customers. Towers Perrin consultant Charles Cornwell comments: "Companies that can properly identify customer expectations and then give their employees the ability to satisfy customers are the ones who are achieving competitive advantage."[3]

The best way to enlist employee support for quality/service improvement programs, according to respondents to the survey, is to institute direct employee involvement with customers, such as visiting customers, having customers meet with employees, and reading customer opinions.

There is one final issue that must be faced. It may be necessary to weed out employees who don't fit in a customer-centered organization. There are two types of employees who leave the organization with no choice: those who just don't get it, and those who get it but just don't buy it. Recently, some educators have come to the conclusion that they should expel students who are disruptive in class. It is, they believe, the only way to be fair to teachers who are there to teach and students who are there to learn. Harsh to be sure, but done in the interest of the greater good.

One way to avoid the problem of employees who consciously or unconsciously diminish customer satisfaction is to exercise care in hiring. Southwest Airlines, which shines as a beacon of customer satisfaction, has its frontline employees screen applicants based on whether they think the candidates will do a good job of customer relations. It is a tough gauntlet to run.

Who are the star performers on the front lines? Harvard Business School Professor Len Schlesinger and consultant Bill Fromm wrote a book on the subject, entitled *The Real Heroes of Business . . . and Not a CEO Among Them.* Of the stars, they said, "Despite differences in age, experience, and education, the common thread is that they are all performers who bring to their work an inspiration that comes from more than a paycheck or a list of goals. Their superior performance is much more than smiles; they all bring intrinsic qualities to the job—like empathy and patience—that cannot be taught."[4]

Schlesinger and Fromm advise companies to look for people who have the energy and interest to expand their own areas of responsibility continuously. The customer service stars, they say, grasp this instinctively. They act as consultants to their customers and have confidence that investing in a long-term relationship with the customer ultimately pays off. Service providers focus on the transaction; *service performers* remain focused on the customer.

# References

1. James L. Heskett, Thomas O. Jones, Gary W. Loveman, W. Earl Sasser, Jr., and Leonard A. Schlesinger, "Putting the Service-Profit Chain to Work," *Harvard Business Review* (March-April 1994).
2. Ibid., p. 169.
3. *Business Wire* release (11/7/94), reprinted in *Positive Impact*, Vol. 5, No. 12 (December 1994).
4. Len Schlesinger and Bill Fromm, *The Real Heroes of Business . . . and Not a CEO Among Them* (New York: Doubleday, 1994).

# 14

# Finance

In some ways, customer satisfaction and finance may seem to be strange bedfellows, but they are not. An enlightened finance department is the information nerve center of an organization, or it should be. Usually, finance people are trained in statistics and information systems, the building blocks of customer satisfaction measurement.

The problem is, finance departments tend to be locked in to archaic accounting principles. For example, there are no provisions in accounting for assigning value to a customer base, nor to employees. Arguably, these are the two greatest assets any company can have. Add to that the inability of accounting to calculate a value for intellectual property and you begin to wonder just how relevant traditional accounting systems are in today's business world.

Accounting is also very limited as a diagnostic tool. It can tell you sales are down, but not why. It can tell you margins are shrinking, but not what to do about it. It can tell you how much better off you would be with more market share, but not how to take it away from your competitors. Compounding the problem is the built-in lag inherent in accounting's score-keeping function. A sale is the culmination of a chain of decisions and events that may go back months or years, but none of that shows up on the books until money changes hands. The figures on an operating statement are a pale, one-dimensional shadow of what is really happening in an organization. And a balance sheet is a step or two removed from that.

It doesn't have to be that way. And it's not necessary to wait for the Financial Accounting Standards Board to find solutions either. It is within the power of any organization to set up its own measuring systems that turn static accounting numbers into something more like moving, three-dimensional holograms with color and sound.

The art of management has been described as asking the right questions. An organization that sees the value in integrating finance and customer satisfaction should start by thinking about what kinds of information and knowledge are needed for effective decision making. This is a distinctly different point of view from being concerned about how to improve accounting procedures.

The health care morass is an example of how point of view can make a difference. Any tinkering with the existing system gores someone's ox, emotions rise, motives are questioned, and finally character assassination sets in. The real issues become obscured in all of the sound and fury. How different it would be to step back and ask a simple question: What would a health care system look like if you were to start with a clean slate, to design the very best medical services delivery to the public without compromising quality yet at the lowest cost? In such a thought process, nothing would be kept sacrosanct.

Can there be any doubt that a system designed through that process would be quite different from today's health care system, with its billions of dollars in waste, fraud, and bitter struggles between competing interests? Impossible, you say. Political and practical realities, entrenched power, and firm tradition would thwart any such effort. Nonetheless, there is value in an unfettered thought process to model the best way to do something. It becomes a goal, something to work toward. As the cliché goes, if you don't know where you're going any road will take you there. If you do know where to go, it helps when *you* choose the route. In the health care analogy, knowing where we were going would make the decisions along the way a lot easier. We don't, and they aren't.

What, then, are the right questions to ask about finance and customer satisfaction? What information does an organization need to make fact-based decisions about control and resource allocation? After all, these are the essential functions of finance—questions often dealt with simplistically, to the peril of those who see it thus.

# Control

There is a great deal more to controlling an organization than turning the money spigot on and off, a technique that has been referred to as diagnostic control. This is the system that measures financial goals and profitability, and progress toward targets such as revenue growth and market share. Executives who believe they can rely on diagnostic controls to keep things on track while they turn their attention elsewhere often pay a terrible price for their naïveté.

In response to reward and punishment systems based on diagnostic controls, managers in the field sometimes resort to manipulation of financial data or consumer scams that blow up in the face of the company. Sears' auto repair business had its knuckles rapped by the courts for a transgression of this kind.

Another form of control is the organization's belief system. Whether written or not, organizations tend to have established patterns of acceptable behavior. Effective managers do a good job of communicating core values and missions that guide employees in their daily decision making and activities. Belief systems can be both positive and negative. Negative beliefs take the form of minimum standards that are the stops that keep people from bending the rules in pursuit of superior results. The standards reflect strict boundaries of morality and behavior that everyone understands must never be crossed. They are enforced clearly and unambiguously.

Finally, there are interactive controls that reach beyond diagnostics. This is the realm of constantly changing information that demands attention, analysis, and discussion—such things as new thrusts by competitors, technological breakthroughs, lurches away from forecast, changes in the economy. In virtually every enterprise, it is possible to identify critical success factors that can be monitored daily, even hourly. Interaction across functional boundaries is the appropriate response to changes in critical success factors.

Even with all of these controls in place and used effectively, managers are kidding themselves if they believe they have all the information they need. For the most part, the customer has been excluded from control-based thinking. And the customer, after all, is the most potent force to be considered. It is the customer who decides whether the organization is doing its job. Peter Drucker had it right more than two decades ago when he wrote: "To know what a business is we have to start with its *purpose*. Its purpose must lie outside of the business itself. In fact, it must lie in society since business enterprise is an organ of society. There is only one valid definition of business purpose: *to create a customer*."[1]

Some final thoughts on control. Old methods of control were firmly in place when the Soviet Union unexpectedly disintegrated. Society has become so complex that it cannot *be* controlled; it must control

itself, employing many of the same, mysterious processes that are ob-
servable in nature.

In his book *Out of Control: The Rise of Neo-Biological Civilization*,
Kevin Kelly, executive editor of *Wired* magazine, describes control in
an age of chaos. He talks about networks that function through a logic
of their own that is unanticipated by their designers. He describes bio-
logical systems that not only change but change how they change, or-
ganizing around self-changing rules.

In the *Harvard Business Review*, William C. Taylor had this to say
about Kelly's paean to biology: "It offers an alluring vision for businesspeople trying to navigate a world marked by accelerating change, un-
forgiving competition, and democratic participation. At their best, natural systems are self-generating and self-organizing; they thrive on
individual choice and spontaneous creativity. At the same time, they
are robust, capable not only of stability but also of self-renewal. And
isn't that the promise of the New Economy? We want companies that
are distributed, decentralized, and collaborative. We also want companies that are enduring and adaptive, capable of healthy change without
violent turmoil."[2]

# Resource Allocation

The second basic function of a finance department is to preserve and
allocate capital resources. The chief financial officer typically sits at the
right hand of the chief executive officer at budgeting time, helping
decide what the company can afford and who should get money for
what purposes. This is not intended as a criticism of any class of professionals, but often the budget process can be described only as mindless.

What conceivable sense does it make to decide, as many companies
do, that advertising expenditures are determined as a percent of sales—
as if sales caused advertising? What is the logic for allowing an across-
the-board increase in budgets by $X$ percent, say the rate of inflation,
when the dynamic influences on line items in a budget are many and
varied? Why would you want to budget for a function on an annual
basis and then divide it by twelve to establish a monthly budget allocation, when the need for cash for that function varies cyclically from
month to month? Why would you treat profit as what's left over rather
than establishing a reasonable profit goal and making the budget fit
the goal?

It is not unusual for budget decisions to be made solely on the basis of management peccadilloes. In the early days of Control Data Corporation, there was a budget meeting at which managers presented ambitious requests for new equipment. As the story goes, founder Bill Norris got progressively more agitated. He is reputed finally to have slammed a fist on the table and said, "You guys are forgetting the first rule of entrepreneuring: Conserve the f***ing cash!"

Resource allocation decisions should be made as though the customer were sitting at the table. If it's the customers who decide whether you're going to be successful or not, wouldn't you want to factor them into any function as critical as budgeting? The issue, of course, is how to do it. Imagine a situation in which management has $1 million to allocate to capital spending over and above fixed expense. Requests submitted by various departments total $1.75 million. Should the decisions be based on the track records of the requesting departments? The persuasiveness of the executives? The "feel" for the business that top management brings to the table? An across-the-board percentage allocation (everybody gets 56.6 percent of what they asked for)? Or some combination of these and other factors?

There is a far better way. Develop a research model that identifies the factors in your customer relationships that have the strongest impact on customer satisfaction. This can be done with a combination of surveys, focus groups, and statistical analysis using multiple regression (a process for testing factors to determine their impact).

The data from such research can be displayed as a performance/importance grid. This is a good first step, but it can lead to flawed decisions unless it is matched with comparative data on competitors. It could be that your company gets a less-than-satisfactory rating on a factor, say delivery, but is still doing better than your competitors are.

It is also important to pay attention to the relative importance of factors in the minds of customers. For example, companies have been known to spend millions on technology to reduce order cycle time from one week to forty-eight hours—when customers were perfectly happy with one-week deliveries but really wanted orders shipped complete. Out-of-stocks are another important dissatisfier that companies might overlook completely.

It is possible to integrate the concepts of importance and performance to produce a ranking of data that is helpful in decision making. This is done by multiplying relative-importance figures by calculated mean competitive difference. Such a calculation might show, for example, that customer service is much more important than changes in product design.

Let's return to management's dilemma in allocating its $1 million.

We can match the requests from the departments with data showing the factors most important to customers and the company's relative standing on these factors compared to competition. Now, additional factors can be entered into the equation. What are the costs of various solutions? The time required for them to become effective? Risks? The anticipated impact on customer satisfaction?

For example, there may be two options for improving customer service: add and train employees, at a cost of $250,000; or introduce new technology, at a cost of $400,000. Once it has been decided that improvements in customer service are the best way to use resources, traditional financial analysis techniques determine which approach is the better investment.

One way to make certain that customer satisfaction gets factored into financial decisions is to put a financially trained executive in charge of customer satisfaction. That's what IBM did at its Baldrige Award-winning facility in Rochester, Minnesota, where Randy Quint, former chief financial officer, became director of quality (which included customer satisfaction). It wasn't long before Quint calculated that a one percent increase in customer satisfaction represented a revenue opportunity of $275 million for IBM. That's the kind of information that rivets top management's attention.

There is one aspect of customer satisfaction measurement that is particularly appealing to numbers-oriented finance executives. An effective measurement system produces results quickly to help evaluate how well changes are working in the marketplace. It's the immediate feedback that is lacking in traditional financial reporting, which is historical and a lagging indicator.

Even the most prescient marketing experts can be dead wrong when it comes to predicting how consumers will react to new products, advertising, and other marketing variables. Their answer is to test, test, test. That's why food companies have test kitchens and taste panels. A sensitive system of organizational telemetry, that is, customer satisfaction measurement, responds very quickly to any changes in the way a company does business. Is a price increase having a deleterious effect? How are consumers reacting to a new product, new packaging, or a new service? Is the new advertising campaign getting through? Is the automated phone system being accepted? How are the new salespeople doing?

Organizational telemetry can be compared to the control room for a power plant, with its panorama of gauges, instruments, and indicators. The operators are only passively concerned with what is going right. But they want to know immediately, by means of horns, bells, or flashing lights, when something is wrong. Like power plant operators, top executives need to know immediately when things are out of kilter so damage can be controlled and changes made.

In *Customer Satisfaction Measurement and Management*, authors Earl Naumann and Kathleen Giel make a statement that should resonate with chief financial officers and their bosses: "Being customer-driven means using the customer to drive continuous improvement, organizational reinvention, and radical redesign. Customer-driven means appointing the customer to be the judge of a firm's value-added processes. The ultimate measure of customer-driven performance is made by customer satisfaction measurement."[3]

Dennis Dammerman, chief financial officer of GE, who tends some $200 billion in assets and annual cash flow of over $6 billion by a recent count, says, "We as finance people have to recognize that there are more measurements than machine output per labor hour, or contribution margin on widget A. There's a whole range of things that are becoming more and more important to managing the business." Dammerman states flatly, "If I could have only two measurements, the two I would choose would be customer satisfaction and cash flow."

Michael J. McConnell, strategy consultant at Deloitte & Touche, cautions against "the danger of mistaking accounting measures for reality." He says most financial systems are several generations behind the times. His advice: "Just as the *Titanic* needed sonar to detect icebergs, senior executives need new concepts and new technology to survive in the treacherous waters of global competition. They need navigation systems that help them respond effectively to changing marketplace realities and that scan a vast horizon for obstacles and opportunities."

# References

1. Peter Drucker *Management Tasks, Responsibilities, Practices* (New York: Harper & Row, 1973).
2. William C. Taylor, "Books in Review," *Harvard Business Review* (November-December 1994), p. 64.
3. Earl Naumann and Kathleen Giel, *Customer Satisfaction Measurement and Management* (Cincinnati, Ohio: Thomason Executive Press, 1995), p. iii.

# 15
# Marketing

Perhaps no area of business is likely to be hit by greater shock waves of change in the next few years than marketing. The reason is that as it has been taught and practiced in the postwar period, marketing has been *mass* marketing, an idea whose time is passing.

The marketing of the future will consider people as individuals, not as mass-migrating lemmings. This change in perspective rewrites all of the rules. It is being aided and abetted by technology on the point of being limited only by imagination.

Marketing is defined as the act of buying and selling, and everything that affects it. Peter Drucker describes marketing as "the whole business seen from the point of view of its final result, that is, from the customer's point of view. Concern and responsibility for marketing must, therefore, permeate all areas of the enterprise."[1]

Attitudes about *sales and marketing*, three words often slurred together as though they were one, have gone through distinct cycles. In the era before business management became professionalized, the sales department was viewed as responsible for selling whatever the factory produced. That attitude evolved into today's idea of producing what the market wants, or at least what it is believed to want.

Selling, as a subfunction under the marketing umbrella, also changed. There was the era of the shoeshine and smile, in which salespeople were trained to be as clever as possible in manipulating customers into buying. More recently, selling has been transformed into trying to understand the psychology of why people buy. The salesperson's assignment has become responding to what the customer wants.

The importance of data has ebbed and flowed through these cycles. Before professional marketing came into its own, the only data that mattered were financial and unit counts on what was chunking out at the end of the line. Then came market-share calculations, sliced ever thinner—territory by territory, state by state, county by county, city by city, neighborhood by neighborhood, store by store.

A new level of sophistication entered the arena with the terms *demographic* and *psychographic*. Not only were customers and prospects being counted, but now they were slotted into categories by sex, age, race, marital status, income, type of residence. Then came lifestyle analysis and personality profiling. The math started getting pretty complicated.

Coupled with the interest in consumer behavior was a growing ability to measure the reach and effectiveness of media. It became possible to calculate exposures, how many times an advertising message is seen or heard. This led to the mathematical exotica of cost-effectiveness.

A Niagara of marketing data became available to companies resourceful enough to be able to use it. In general, marketers knew what was happening but not necessarily why. Marketing people knew that if they spent $X$ dollars on advertising in media $Y$, sales would amount to $Z$ dollars. But it was a puzzlement whether the most important thing was what advertisers were saying, how they were saying it, where they were saying it, or how loud their voice was.

There is no disputing the effectiveness of mass marketing. It has resulted in an incredible array of products and services available to consumers at competitive prices. It produced the supermarket, discount chains, category killers, and behemoth malls—conveniences few people would willingly give up. It has resulted in giant corporations fueled by billions of dollars in transactions, which provide employment for hundreds of thousands of people. But if mass marketing is so successful, why is it destined to go the way of the dodo? Two reasons: It has become dehumanizing, with the result that people are rebelling. And there is a better way.

History is replete with examples of the irrepressibility of the human spirit: the American revolution to break free from royal excess; the rise of unions in response to the cruelties of industrialization; the decline of unions when they abused their power; the current political rebellion against some of the absurdities of government bureaucracy. In the world of commerce today, there are clear signs that people are not going to put up with dehumanizing practices. They don't have to; they have too many alternatives. They know they can vote with their feet. Communication has raised the general awareness level, clearing away the mists of ignorance and naïveté.

It was the conventional wisdom that purchasers could get quality, or good service, or lowest price, but they had to choose. You couldn't get all three, or in most cases even two. Anyone in business who believes that today is on the brink of disaster. Customers are demanding the world, and if you don't give it to them someone else will. In many businesses, there has been an attitude that a lost customer is no big deal; there will be another one along any minute. Auto dealers were notorious for this kind of cynical disregard for the individual, but they weren't alone.

Mass marketing, with its emphasis on numbers rather than the flesh-and-blood people who are the reality behind the numbers, has led to insensitive practices and the shoulder-shrugging indifference of frontline employees who deal with the public. It has led to the isolation of management from the people they are supposed to be serving.

In many companies, a shockingly high percentage of employees spend their entire careers without *ever* communicating on a human level with the customers whose buying decisions keep the enterprise going. Is it any wonder these employees become detached, disinterested, and incapable of serving the best interests of customers? What is the better way? What will the marketing world of the future look like?

It will be a logical extension of everything learned through the era of mass marketing. It will build on the past, but not replace it.

Here is how mass marketing looks at a customer:

> He is male; age thirty-two; has a master's degree in sociology; is heterosexual and married with two children, a boy and a girl; is a homeowner who lives in zip code 55391; is computer literate; plays golf and tennis; holds a corporate job in a mid-size company; earns $42,000 a year; drives a Chevrolet Cavalier purchased new; drinks moderately and doesn't smoke; goes to church regularly; prefers classical music; has a cellular phone, three television sets (views TV 1.6 hours daily), one computer at home with a CD-ROM drive and American Online; subscribes to cable; and reads *Atlantic Monthly, Business Week,* and the daily newspaper. Finally, he is slotted into the statistics of whatever the inquiring company's interest is: our man as a customer, a prospect, or a suspect.

The people-oriented marketer of the future looks at all of the information described above and says, "That's a start." Here is what is added: name, spelled correctly; a calculation of the lifetime value of this person as a customer; some grasp of what this person's life is like (dreams, problems, attitudes, future needs, satisfiers, dissatisfiers); and information on when and how best to make contact at a human level in order to develop a relationship. "But that's too hard," you may be saying; "we can't do all of that. It would be too costly. It would price us out of the market." Or: "It's too complicated; we wouldn't know how to begin." Nor could the people who designed the '56 Chevy have told you at that time how to design a car with all of the features and capabilities of today's Lexus, either. The seemingly impossible comes about through continuous improvement . . . when you set your sights high enough.

As an example of how far marketing has advanced from conventional mass marketing practices, selected subscribers to *Fortune* recently had this experience. Their magazine fell open to an insert: an invitation from Lexus for a test drive, with their name printed on the invitation. Included was a card to take to their Lexus dealer for a selection of attractive gifts valued at $55 in return for taking a test drive.

This says a mouthful to the customer. It says Lexus knows them by name and values them as a potential customer. It recognizes the value of the customer's time by offering a gift for taking the time to go to a dealer. It treats the potential customer with respect and appreciation, indicating the kind of relationship customers can expect from their Lexus dealer.

Behind that kind of promotion, no doubt, Lexus is thinking of lifetime value rather than the profit from a single transaction. The auto industry has calculated the lifetime value of a customer at something like $300,000. That gives the number crunchers some serious money to work with. Surely Lexus also knows the close rate on test drives, so that factor can be entered into the calculations. *Fortune* has good demographics on its readers, so it is probably able to make a pretty good match with Lexus data on who buys cars in the Lexus class. The result is a reasonable projection of how many *Fortune* subscribers will respond to the test-drive offer and purchase a Lexus.

In an article on customer service, *Inc.* magazine invited readers to let their imagination run wild. "Suppose your company could really satisfy its customers. Suppose you could provide a product or service that was better than they expected, for less money than anybody else charged. Suppose that every time you brought out something new it was just what buyers wanted. Suppose your after-sale service was so good that customers with problems went away feeling better than before." The article continued, "What would happen? Easy—you'd own your marketplace. People would buy from you over and over again, would relish the experience, would never even dream about doing business with anybody else. They would proselytize on your behalf, telling their friends and associates to buy from you. You'd hardly need salespeople."[2]

The magazine went on to explain that the description was not of an imaginary company. It was the real world of Intuit, developer of Quicken, the dominant consumer and small business cash management software for personal computers. Intuit founder Scott Cook, a Harvard MBA and former Procter & Gamble marketer, was from the very start in 1983 a fanatic about understanding customers. As a result, Intuit did in fact come to own its marketplace. Convincing demonstration of this fact came with Microsoft's 1995 offer of $2 billion for Intuit, a rather smallish company. Microsoft was deeply disappointed when the justice department put the kibosh on the deal. Microsoft knows it will be almost impossible and hugely expensive to dislodge the loyal users of Quicken.

It is no surprise that Intuit does the usual customer satisfaction measurement things: an annual customer survey, asking which of Quicken's features buyers use and don't use, like and don't like; anonymous polls of dealers, asking what personal-finance programs they recommend and why; compilation of data from customers who call in with problems or write in with suggestions; focus groups, usually consisting of people who aren't Quicken customers but ought to be.

But Intuit doesn't stop there. They created a program called Follow-Me-Home, in which buyers of Quicken are asked to let an Intuit representative observe them when they unwrap the software at home and first install it on their computer. Intuit representatives are known to spend as much as five hours with a customer, returning to the company with a pad full of notes on how Quicken could be made a bit easier for first-time users.

British Airways, by looking at its service from the customer's perspective, adopted an entirely different approach to first-class transatlantic service from its competitors. While most airlines were promoting lavish food service, BA found that passengers mostly just wanted to sleep and were concerned as much about what happens on the ground as in the air. BA gives premium fliers the option of dinner on the ground in the first-class lounge. Once they get on board, they can slip into BA pajamas if they wish, put their heads on real pillows, curl up under a duvet, and then enjoy an interruption-free flight. On arrival, well-rested passengers can have breakfast, use comfortable dressing rooms and shower stalls, and even have their clothes pressed before they leave for business. The result: BA profits were up 61 percent after the new services were offered.

The most advanced marketing ideas have usually come from the consumer-oriented retail businesses. The industrial sector typically has lagged behind, focusing more on product than on customer. Industrial companies spend far less on marketing, and as a rule they haven't attracted the flashier marketing talent. That makes the thinking at SKF North America all the more remarkable, considering that the company produces bearings. SKF chief Raymond Langton says, "In today's world, to retain business you cannot look at it as if you were selling a product. You are providing a value-added service."

What does that mean? SKF works with its customers to ensure that they mount and maintain bearings properly in order to reduce downtime at their plants. Langton watches the turnover rate of key corporate accounts and distributors like a hawk and considers it equally as important as market share. "If you are constantly churning accounts," he observes, "you aren't selling on value-added service. You are selling on price."[3]

The rallying cry for the future in marketing circles is likely to be *customer retention.* The conventional wisdom is that a 5 percent decrease in customer defection rates increases profits by a minimum of 25 percent. It's easy to accept that figure when you consider that revenues and market share feed on repeat sales and referrals. Costs fall because it isn't necessary to spend heavily to replace defectors. While loyal customers expect a good price, value is most important to them. Price then filters out fickle buyers who jump back and forth for pennies. Increased customer retention improves employee morale, which cuts employee turnover, which in turn improves productivity and lowers operating costs.

Another tidbit of conventional wisdom is that it costs five times as much to attract a new customer as it does to retain one you already have. Can it be more obvious that companies should allocate the lion's share of resources to customer retention? Yet most companies take their customers for granted—especially their best customers. When the big account is canceled, top management leaps into action trying to save it. Often they are chagrined to realize they haven't talked to anybody at that account for years. At that point, of course, it's too late.

Management not only takes customers for granted; they set up systems that motivate everyone else in the company to do so also. Executives get paid out of all proportion to their value for hyping quar-

terly results, while doing irreparable harm to the customer and employee base. Salespeople are given incentives for opening new accounts, but nothing for account retention. Executives get promoted for
growing sales, but there is no recognition for the quality of those sales.
Huge sums are allocated for sales and promotion activities, but very
little for customer service, which is viewed as a necessary expense
rather than a profit generator. Customer service people are rewarded
for volume of activity rather than level of empathy with customers, the
result being abruptness and disinterest. Quality takes the first hit when
budget cutting becomes necessary.

In a gradual reversal of these self-defeating practices, companies
are beginning to accept these precepts:

- Service is more important than products. As much as 80 percent
  of customer dissatisfaction comes in the area of the relationship
  rather than product. It's clear where the emphasis needs to be
  in order to achieve customer loyalty.
- The old idea of a vendor is passé. In the future, companies that
  buy and sell to each other will think of themselves as partners
  and act accordingly. This means a degree of openness and mutual reliance that is distinctly uncomfortable for traditionalists
  who like to play it close to the vest.
- It is necessary to live the life of your customer. No amount of
  cool, antiseptic research can take the place of being with your
  customers on their firing line. In Native American wisdom, "To
  know a man, walk a mile in his moccasins."
- Employees are not disposable. To retain customers, the first emphasis must be on retaining employees. Businesses that take
  high employee turnover for granted are the same ones that do
  poorly at building customer loyalty: banks, auto dealerships,
  retailing, restaurants. It doesn't have to be that way.

# References

1. Peter Drucker, *Management* (New York: Harper & Row, 1973), p.63.
2. John Case, "Customer Service: The Last Word," *Inc.* (April 1991).
3. Rahul Jacob, "Why Some Customers Are More Equal Than Others,"
   *Fortune* (September 1994), p. 215.

# 16

# Product Development

Development of new products and services is a dicey business. It is expensive. Failure rates can be horrendous. It takes longer than most executives would like. Most frustrating of all, competitors seem to be good at it. But it isn't as if there were any choice. If you want to stay in business you have to develop new offerings, and do it as well as possible.

You would expect that anything so important, and so challenging, would be fully organized and accomplished efficiently in most companies. You would be wrong. There are essentially two reasons why companies have difficulty with new product development. First, virtually every department of a company is affected by or involved in some way with new products, yet communications between departments is abysmal. Boundaries are very real. Functional areas operate as though they were watertight compartments. By its nature, product development should cross boundaries easily, but in many companies it simply cannot. The result: conflict, inefficiency, cross purposes, dropped balls, sabotage, stalled creativity, and discouragement.

Second, the voice of the customer seldom is heard loudly and clearly by all of the people involved in product development decision making. And of course it's the customer who ultimately determines whether new products and services succeed or fail. The mechanisms for recording and amplifying the voice of the customer are often lacking or poorly developed.

# Dissolving Issues That
# Block Product Development

When organizations make a determined effort to become customer-centered and work hard at the cultural change incumbent upon the decision, the issues that block effective new product development tend to dissolve.

In the 1995 Industrial Design Excellence Awards competition, Thomson Consumer Electronics, which acquired RCA products in 1988 and has consistently improved their style and quality, walked off with four medals because of the consideration it gave to consumers in designing its ProScan line of TV sets. Instruction books for technical products are notoriously user unfriendly— obtuse gobbledygook written by underpaid and poorly qualified technical writers. Recognizing that the instruction manual, the first thing consumers pick up after their proud purchase, makes a priceless first impression, Thomson assembled a team of cognitive psychologists, creative writers, and engineers to write a new guidebook.

ProScan has many features that are marvels of electronic wizardry. Thomson wanted users to try them out, so along with an easy-to-understand manual the company developed icons similar to those found on a PC. Selecting the graphic guides with the remote control, viewers can perform dozens of tasks easily, such as changing picture quality, programming viewing menus, and getting answers to questions. A complicated remote control, the bane of anyone old enough to vote, was eliminated. ProScan's remote control has only eight buttons, compared to the forty-plus found on an average remote. It controls power, channel changing, and volume, plus the on-screen graphic menu, all with a point-and-select feature. Based on suggestions from one hundred prospective customers, the remote is shaped to rest easily in the palm.

The jury for the awards said it was most impressed by the Thomson team's efforts to consider the human factor. "They worked really hard at making it easy for the customer to use," said one of the judges.[1] It is remarkable that a design contest judge would find that a designer thinking about the customer was worthy of note.

# Perpetual Renewal With
# Consumer-Friendly Products

Another example of intense devotion to the consumer is a company that for the past two years has headed *Fortune's* list of America's most admired companies: Rubbermaid. The company is perpetually renewing itself through a prodigious cornucopia of consumer-friendly new products. It has been called a product juggernaut. "Our objective," says CEO Wolfgang Schmitt, "is to bury competitors in such a profusion of products that they can't copy us." To do that, Rubbermaid introduces as many as three hundred new products per year. The goal is for at least 33 percent of any year's total sales to come from products introduced in the previous five years.

One of the ways they do it is by breaking down traditional departmental barriers. Researchers, designers, manufacturing people, and marketers function together as business teams. Their mandate is to generate ideas and get products to market as quickly as possible. Executives are encouraged to read customer letters, visit stores, and listen to focus groups and user panels. For product testing, Rubbermaid employs consumer and user groups extensively and follows them with in-home testing.

The effort is not confined to end users. Rubbermaid also considers retailers as customers and pays extraordinary attention to them. Retail managers are invited to Rubbermaid headquarters at the rate of three per week. Product managers use these visits to describe ideas under development and get reaction. The lively discussions with the retailers include talk about consumer trends, promotional opportunities, product strengths and weaknesses, store layouts, pricing, and packaging. Discussions like this help make Rubbermaid business teams sensitive to issues of importance to retailers, such as how products stack on shelves and merchandising considerations.

Rubbermaid also gets involved with higher-level executives from retail organizations, inviting them from time to time to meet with senior executives of Rubbermaid. These discussions run to such issues as how to integrate computer systems for faster ordering, delivery, and billing. At these meetings, there tends to be a focus on longer-range strategy.

Rubbermaid is featured in a book on *Product Juggernauts* by two Arthur D. Little consultants, Jean-Philippe Deschamps and P. Ranganath Nayak. They say the key to constant creation of world-class products is to develop competencies across every function in the organization. The result at Rubbermaid, they say, is 500–900 new product ideas generated per year, of which 350– 400 get implemented and introduced. Of these, more than 90 percent are market successes, "an astonishing hit rate in the fiercely competitive, mass-volume consumer goods market."[2]

There are many factors in Rubbermaid's high new-product success rate. The company has earned the trust and loyalty of end users and retailers. Loyal customers are accepting of new products and new technologies. A seasoned sales force knows the product area and the needs, the concerns and requirements of both customers and channels of distribution. Newcomers to a market enjoy none of these advantages.

## Measuring Trust and Loyalty

In a complete customer satisfaction measurement system, elements such as the trust and loyalty of end users and channels are measured consistently. The effectiveness of the sales force is also quantified. Strengths in these areas have a profound positive effect on new product development; weaknesses have a profound negative effect.

Before companies allocate significant resources to the development and introduction of new products, they would do well to take the pulse of the customer satisfaction attributes that in the end determine whether the product can succeed and what it takes in the way of promotional and distribution horsepower to achieve that success.

The most colorful business consultants stimulate the imagination by portraying the marketplace as a cross between a jungle and a barnyard. Companies are encouraged to eat their young, that is, kill off new products to make room for even newer ones. They are discouraged from cannibalizing product lines, setting up their own products so they compete with each other. Cash cows are mature product lines squirting the milk of profits. Dogs are cash eaters that scavenge corporate resources.

In a world as savage as all that—one where, as Intel's Andy Grove contends, "only the paranoid survive"—the best defense is information: Know your strengths and know your weaknesses.

## A Rich Repository of Information

In every organization, there is a department or function that is a rich repository of information about what is going on in the world of the customer. For years, this department or function—customer service—has been thought of as a necessary evil. The most advanced companies are now beginning to see customer service as a mother lode of valuable data. In fact, a survey taken in 1994 indicated that customer service had become the main focus of investments in technology for some 70 percent of large U.S. and European companies. Corporate

America, according to *Business Week,* is spending more than $1 billion a year on computers and related technology for customer service departments.

The money is for the purpose of extracting marketing, sales, and design data from customer-service operations. Until recently, according to *Business Week,* "know the customer" was usually more easily said than done. Computer technology just wasn't up to the job; the data existed but were too voluminous, too widely scattered, and recorded too inconsistently to be useful. "Now," according to the publication, "with high-powered workstations, extensive networks, specialized software packages, and extra-powerful database computers, technology is no longer a problem."[3]

For example, Attachmate Corp., a smallish PC communications software company, gets 165,000 support calls each year. It uses the data to plan enhancements for its established products and give shape to entirely new ones. Vice President Mary Harwood said it gives us "a very clear picture of what's going on in the marketplace."[4]

Otis Elevator redesigns its equipment and improves maintenance procedures based on the 1.2 million calls it gets each year. When equipment failures result in repair calls, a full-time, twenty-member engineering team reviews the incident and any similar cases in the computer to see whether there is a pattern in the failures that warrants redesign, or maybe a new product or service.

At the opposite extreme of customer data being generated through elaborate computerized information systems is the executive who learns how to be observant and translates that discipline into new product ideas. Arnold Hiatt, the retired CEO of the Stride Rite shoe company, became an inveterate foot watcher. He recalls being on a flight from Korea to Hong Kong when he noticed a child wearing shoes with a loop at the top of the heel that made it easier for the parent or child to pull on the shoe. The following season, Stride Rite had a shoe like that in its line, and it was a hit with customers. Said Hiatt, the foot watcher, "I knew that if I based decisions only on information filtered through other people, the possibility of those decisions being accurate was diminished. To make informed decisions, you should base them not just upon what you know, but what you see."[5] Hiatt takes pride in personally never losing touch with customers while annual sales have grown from $40 million to over $550 million.

At Oil Changers, a forty-unit California chain of quick oil-change shops, CEO Larry Read insists that each of his twenty-six corporate employees spend one day a month working in a company shop. They then get together for a monthly round table to discuss what they've seen and heard at the stores and ideas for improvements.

## Listening to Customers Can Be Tricky

It should be noted that the business of listening to customers can be tricky, and in some cases disastrously misleading. Just ask Coca-Cola about New Coke, which tested well with consumers but sold poorly. Same thing goes for McDonald's McLean hamburger. And when Chrysler came up with the idea for the minivan, market research found customers to be distinctly unimpressed with what to them was an odd-looking vehicle. Fortunately for Chrysler, the company thought it knew better than the customers and forged ahead, to a resounding success.

*Fortune* published an article on this subject with the attention-getting headline "Ignore Your Customers." It was a cautionary tale about the danger in "becoming a feedback fanatic, slavishly devoted to customers, constantly trying to get in even better touch through more focus groups, more surveys. Not only can that distract you from the real work at hand," *Fortune* suggested, "but it may also cause you to create new offerings that are safe and bland."[6]

The issue really is not ignoring customers; that would be stupid. The issue is understanding them so well that you know when they don't really mean what they say. The way to do that, to the greatest degree possible, is through multiple channels of information, first-hand observation, and the exercise of that most uncommon of qualities, common sense.

Visionaries sometimes find themselves standing up to play-it-safe corporate bureaucrats, statisticians, and marketing "experts" armed with consumer research. The ones whose faith was strong enough to prevail have writ their names large in business history. *Fortune* gives these examples: "George Foerstner, president of Amana, who, back in the 1960s, believed in the value of microwave ovens, even when most consumers thought them bizarre, even dangerous. Or take Clarence 'Bob' Birdseye, the father of frozen food. When he started peddling his idea in 1922, he met with acrimony from food retailers who didn't want to install expensive freezer equipment and from consumers who distrusted the quality of his products. At one point he had 1.6 million pounds of unsold frozen fish on his hands. But he ignored his critics, and by the 1940s frozen food had become a staple."[7]

# Anthropological Market Research

The idea of paying only scant attention to what people say, and a great deal of attention to what they do, now has a name that may put it in the pantheon of business buzzwords—not yet but maybe someday. It's called *anthropological market research,* after the science of studying folkways.

A dedicated user of the technique is Steelcase, the office furniture manufacturer. The company sets up video cameras in work environments and exhaustively analyzes the tapes, looking for the patterns of behavior and motion that customers themselves don't even notice. It then designs its furniture to accommodate the way people actually work.

Urban Outfitters, a chain of clothing stores, also videotapes customers in their native habitats, as well as in stores. The resulting "customer profiles" give managers and merchandisers a feel for what people are actually wearing and allow the company to make quick decisions on merchandise. It just so happens that the president of Urban Outfitters, Richard Hayne, was an anthropology major. "We're not after people's statements," he says, "we're after their actions."[8]

Concludes *Fortune* in its cleverly titled article: "At the end of the day, everything a company does—even down to ignoring its customers—must ultimately be met with customer approval. If a company truly understands its customers' needs, it can in good conscience disregard what they claim to want. This will save you lots of time, not to mention aggravation and some potentially embarrassing moves. Ignore your customers. They'll thank you for it in the end."[9]

There should obviously be a linkage between customer satisfaction measurement and product development. Yet in many companies the linkage is tenuous at best. New product designers tend to be supremely confident that they know what customers want. They are often disdainful of number-crunching market researchers. Marketing people, schooled in and dedicated to the fast-becoming-passé techniques of mass marketing, rarely leave their cubicles to deal with customers as fellow human beings. Top management often is so far removed from the hurly-burly of the marketplace that judgment and instincts are dulled into ineffectiveness. Financial executives find it difficult to look beyond the bloodless numbers to understand the whole new realm of measurements available to take the pulse of an organization in real time.

Companies that are not satisfied with the output of their new product development process should start by correcting the two obstacles mentioned at the beginning of this chapter. The solution to departmental isolation and insulation is the cross-functional team, an example of which is found at Rubbermaid. And injecting the voice of the customer into the process starts with the creation of effective customer satisfaction measurement methods, as with Urban Outfitters. In most organizations, neither of these obstacles can be overcome meaningfully without a concerted program of cultural change.

# References

1. Kevin Kelly, "Annual Design Awards," *Business Week* (June 5, 1995).
2. Jean-Philippe Deschamps and P. Ranganath Nayak, *Product Juggernauts* (Boston: Harvard Business School Press, 1995).
3. John W. Verity, "The Gold Mine of Data in Customer Service," *Business Week* (March 21, 1994), p. 113.
4. Ibid., p. 114.
5. Donna Fenn, "Street Smart," *Profit* (November-December 1994), p. 37.
6. Justin Martin, "Ignore Your Customers," *Fortune* (May 1995), p. 121.
7. Ibid., p. 124.
8. Ibid., p. 125.
9. Ibid., p. 126.

# 17

# Customer Service

Ask most executives about their organization's customer service strategy, and they will respond with pabulum about courtesy, response time, and guaranteed satisfaction. If you point out that such things do not represent a strategy, it may end the conversation.

These same executives spend little time thinking about customer service. They view it as a department or function, where the phone gets answered (after negotiating voice mail), orders are taken, information is given, repair people are dispatched, or complaints are handled. A log of how these executives spend their time would show few activities related to customer service. As a function, it is usually so submerged organizationally that it may not even show up as a line item at budget time. It reports to somebody, who reports to somebody, who reports to somebody.

## Some Executives Monitor Customer Service

A few executives point out that they monitor customer service by talking with customers. Some say they disguise their voices and call in to the company every now and then to see what it's like to be a customer (not a bad idea).

In business, the spotlight of attention shines most brightly on the product. Design it, finance it, produce it, advertise it, sell it, distribute it. Even in such service businesses as banking and securities, they talk about products. The very identity of employees is wrapped up in how they relate to *the product,* and they are rewarded and recognized in proportion to how well the product sells.

On reflection, this is curious. There is common understanding that we are becoming a service economy, but the facts behind the statement are not fully appreciated. To start with, according to government statistics approximately three-fourths of all U.S. workers are employed in industries regarded as services: communications, transportation, health care, wholesale and retail distribution, financial services, and professional services. Add to that the fact that some 70 percent of those working in manufacturing industries perform service tasks such as research, logistics, maintenance, marketing, design, accounting, law, finance, and personnel functions, and account for three-fourths of all costs. So, it would seem that no matter what you do you are in the service business. Now, one more time: What is your customer service strategy?

The challenge is that if you provide too little service, or the wrong kind, customers will leave; provide too much, even the right kind, and you will go broke or price yourself out of the market.

These are not happy alternatives, but we see them being played out on the pages of the business press every day in stories about companies headed by executives who fail to grasp that the essence of their business, whatever it may seem to be, is really customer service. Some companies attempt to segment customers, choosing which ones to serve, thus improving productivity without imperiling customer satisfaction.

The problem with the term *segmented* is that it smacks of the old mass-marketing mentality that arranges numbers in orderly patterns as though they represented information and knowledge, not merely data. To segment with a semblance of sensitivity requires understanding and awareness of the fundamentals of human behavior.

# The Cattle Prod Approach

Take, for example, First Bank in Chicago. They segmented their customers into those who use ATMs and those who prefer to go to human tellers. (Teller transactions are much more expensive for the bank than ATM transactions.) Wanting to reduce its costs and make more money, the bank decided that the way to get people to use ATMs was to punish them for using tellers by levying a heavy teller transaction charge.

This could be described as the cattle prod approach: If people don't do what you want them to do, hit them with an electric shock. How much better it would have been, and in the end how much more profitable, to simply provide an incentive for using ATMs. For example, ATM users could accrue points for every transaction, redeemable for merchandise, travel, or a percentage off on account charges (the idea behind frequent flyer programs). The result is predictable: Bank customers would feel good about switching from tellers to ATMs and would do so in droves. They would appreciate a new benefit being provided by the bank. The cost of the benefit would be more than offset by the reduction in teller costs, by favorable rather than negative publicity, and by attracting new customers from competitors. And there would be no loss of customers alienated by the cattle prod approach. A win-win, no matter how you figure it.

At the heart of the idea—the necessity of developing a customer service strategy—is the need for a valid, consistent, comprehensive customer satisfaction measurement system. Otherwise organizations are afflicted with management by intuition as opposed to management by fact. This is not to say that intuition is not important; it is just that intuitive leaps bound higher and truer from a pad of facts.

Even the best customer service systems are doomed to deteriorate unless they are supported by an effective measurement system. The world is a passing parade, with changing competitors, customer preferences, technologies, and employee capabilities. Measures establish the feedback loops through which companies learn to respond.

Take, for example, Taco Bell. It entered a world dominated by phenomenally successful McDonald's. The success of McDonald's is attributed to its devotion to quick service, clean surroundings, and uniform products. To achieve these customer-focused objectives, McDonald's used a mass-production approach. Essentially, the mass-production model puts the frontline workers last.

Taco Bell perceived that attracting and retaining today's customers requires a different approach, one that puts the frontline workers first and supports them with the most efficient business systems possible. To do this, Taco Bell restructured its entire organization from top to bottom, creating a new model very different from McDonald's.

The result? Over at the competitors', growth and profitability of McDonald's has slowed. It has become hard to find satisfactory employees. Costs have shot up. Customers have defected to the rivals. It is difficult for McDonald's to respond because it is saddled with a huge infrastructure based on the employee-comes-last model of mass production. Meanwhile, Taco Bell has been growing like Jack's bean stalk. In a relatively flat market, the company achieved growth rates in the 60 percent range. Profits have zoomed 25 percent compared to less than 6 percent at McDonald's. This has been accomplished while prices have been slashed 25 percent, and more cuts are always in the works.

# Comparison of McDonald's and Taco Bell Is Revealing

To understand the difference you need only comparison-shop a McDonald's and a Taco Bell. Taco Bell is every bit as clean and predictable as McDonald's, but the food is less expensive and served faster, and the servers are friendlier and seem more competent. The facility probably isn't as large and fancy, but you don't care. That isn't why you are there.

On investigation, you find that Taco Bell has reversed the polarity of fast-food operations, shifting from manufacturing meals to serving customers. Managers and frontline workers are hired based on their attitudes about responsibility, teamwork, and customer service; and they receive incentive pay, above the industry averages, based on customer satisfaction measurement.

Harvard Business School professor Leonard Schlesinger, who has studied McDonald's and Taco Bell in depth, made this observation: "While all these changes have been taking place at Taco Bell, McDonald's has focused on more of the same: more advertising and promotion efforts, more new products, more new locations. But more of the same no longer works. Competing against Taco Bell and other redesigned service businesses demands a shift in management's mind-set as well as a new appreciation for the real value of service and the value that service employees create."[1]

John E. Martin, president and CEO of Taco Bell, commented: "Taking action is a very frightening proposition for many companies. That is why the vast majority of organizations today continue subscribing to the notion that 'if it's not broken, don't fix it.' If ever there were a cliché that needed to be eradicated from our collective mind-set, this is it.

"The break-it organization places customers at the forefront of every important strategic decision, keeping nimble, flexible, and ready to respond on a moment's notice rather than frozen by paradigms of the past."[2]

Talk about shattering paradigms! Taco Bell, a restaurant chain, decided to virtually get rid of its kitchens. Can you imagine the shocked looks on people's faces when the suggestion was first made? How can you have a restaurant without a kitchen? Martin explains: "Large, mul-tifunctional kitchens did not provide customers with what they wanted most: great food at a great price delivered by people who really cared about their needs. Eliminating the kitchen—a program we call K-mi-nus—enabled us to reduce an expensive operational element that was driving up our prices. Most important, it enabled us to bring many of our employees who once were stuck in the back, shredding lettuce and chopping tomatoes, out to the front where they could serve cus-tomers."[3]

The Taco Bell vs. McDonald's saga illustrates how market condi-tions can change, requiring a change in customer service strategy. The challenge is to understand what consumers really want and value. The example is sometimes given that when cars came only in black, the market appeared to want black cars. But once consumers were given a choice, everything changed forever.

Another example comes from the investment securities field. Back when commissions for securities trading were regulated, the market appeared to want full service, complete with research support and hand-holding. With deregulation came a reshuffling of services. Now, according to a Towers Perrin survey, as much as a third of such trading is handled through discount brokers, another third through mutual fund complexes—many sold on a direct no-load basis—and the re-maining third through full-commission, full-service brokers.

The product in every case is the same: an investment. The variance is in the range of related services. One approach is not superior to another intrinsically. Each is superior for the customer who wants and needs it.

## Understanding the Customer Is Much Discussed in the Insurance Industry

An article in the trade publication *Best's Review* puts understanding the customer in perspective (in an insurance industry context): "Con-sumers define their own hierarchies of wants. They calibrate the value of quality and customer service in relation to alternatives and their particular needs. . . . Insurers must study customer wants in detail. They cannot afford trial and error, a 'we know what's best for our customer' approach or a 'build it and they will come' attitude. . . . Once an insurer understands what its target customers require and how they measure value, the insurer also must understand their economics. It is self-defeating for a company to offer a particular service that delivers less value to the customer than it costs the company to provide it. At the same time, the company should not fail to capitalize on highly valued service that can be delivered cost-effectively."[4]

In the financial world there are risk/reward ratios. In the customer service arena there are equally immutable cost/benefit ratios. While it is easy to understand that there are relationships between risk and reward and between cost and benefit, decision making based on these tradeoffs gets more difficult. Just how difficult is illustrated by the dilemma facing government. In this age of paradox, government is confronted by two very difficult challenges in the areas of reengineering and customer satisfaction. First, there is recognition that government must become more sensitive to customer satisfaction as a part of initiatives to restructure government. A critical part of any customer satisfaction effort is professional and continuing customer satisfaction measurement. The first paradox is this: Restructuring is aimed at and driven by cost reduction; customer satisfaction measurement costs money.

Additionally, the reengineering of government is resulting in elimination of hundreds of thousands of jobs. This can be devastating to the morale of the survivors. The second paradox, then, is this: It is not possible to achieve a high level of customer service and customer satisfaction with a dispirited, disgruntled, unfulfilled workforce. So how can you redesign government and at the same time achieve customer satisfaction?

In government, business, and any other kind of organization, including the vast nonprofit sector of the economy, brain teasers like this bring to mind the saying, "That's why management gets the big bucks." These are not easy choices, but in the end they are dictated by clarity of vision and the strength of underlying principles.

Underlying principle was demonstrated dramatically at the time of the Tylenol poisoning incident. Management unhesitatingly recalled all of its product, at a cost of hundreds of millions of dollars. There was no equivocation. There were no protestations about how it wasn't the company's fault. It was simply a matter of protecting the customer, and, incidentally, the company's reputation. Cost was secondary—not a deciding factor. In the end, of course, the value of the Tylenol brand was protected, and revenues far exceeded the cost of the recall.

A similar case occurred at Honeywell when it was found that under extremely rare circumstances its gas valves in furnaces and space heaters would stick in the open position, causing an explosion. Cost was ruled out as a consideration when the decision was made to recall millions of valves and carry out a complex program of inspection and replacement. The company simply favored its customers over its balance sheet.

# Clarity of Vision Must Go Beyond Simplistic Slogans

To be effective, clarity of vision must be interpreted in down-to-earth language and specifics that can be understood by all employees. Suppose you are in the business of manufacturing doors. You believe your competitive edge can come only by providing better customer service than your competitors. How would you go about communicating this idea? Here's how the Norfield company did it, as reported in a publication of the Doors and Hardware Institute and digested in the newsletter *Positive Impact*:

> It doesn't seem to be enough to offer "quality products at a reasonable price"—everyone tries to do that. But whether you're manufacturing doors or running a lunch counter, the companies who really stand out are those who are committed to excellence in serving their customers.
>
> The focus on excellent customer service begins on the first day an employee reports to work. Beginning with thorough training in product knowledge, the new employee is gearing up to provide knowledgeable assistance to the professionals who comprise [sic] our customer base. Additional training in telephone skills, computer operation, internal paperwork, etc., all add to the overall expertise required for an employee to be able to offer excellent service. Without a commitment to employee training, it is not possible for any company to effectively serve its customers.

Norfield stresses what it calls "The 4 P's of Customer Service."

- Professionalism
- Performance
- Persistence
- Personality

**Professionalism**

Professionalism is more than sounding good on the telephone or even being categorized as a "professional" in a particular field. It includes offering customers a level of expertise that enables them to focus on what they do rather than spending precious time on what you can do for them

Sometimes professionalism in customer service means turning away business! If you know your customer can do better elsewhere or that you are unable to deliver to your customer's requirements, referring them to someone else might be the best way to keep them!

### Performance

Our performance standard is "Zero Defects." Beginning with the design and manufacture of parts and ending with the shipment of customer orders, everyone in the organization shares the same ideal of quality.

Every order placed is confirmed before being finalized to avoid possible errors in input or communication. Also, each customer who is sent a priority package is called to be sure the package arrived as scheduled.

### Persistence

Nothing compares with good, old-fashioned, stick-to-it-ness. In customer service, this can be applied in a number of ways. Sometimes it can mean making three or four phone calls just to be sure an address is correct before a shipment goes out. It can also involve demanding that a vendor meet his commitment so customers receive shipments on time. There is no question that it requires a commitment to quality, to honesty, and to making sure the customer is served well.

### Personality

Everyone likes to have a good time! Why not enjoy what you're doing? It is not at all difficult for customers to pick up on the attitudes of people they're doing business with. Whether someone is having a bad day or has a bad attitude toward their company, the negative energy comes through loud and clear. On the other hand, a smile comes through loud and clear—even over the phone.

Norfield president Bruce Norlie lets his employees know that this is what he tells customers: "Since 1959, we have focused on quality, innovation, and customer service. Our promise is to provide friendly, knowledgeable people to serve you, quality products you need in stock, and fast response. If we are not fulfilling this promise, please call me personally."[5]

That is a nice sentiment, and customers do occasionally take the boss up on invitations of this kind. The problem is most dissatisfied customers don't complain; they just vote with their feet and tell any-body who will listen why they did it. Studies have shown that, as a minimum, for every complaint received there are ten more customers dissatisfied for the same reason who don't complain but just abandon ship.

An important first step in understanding sources of customer dis-satisfaction is to have a process for tracking, measuring, and respond-ing to complaints. It is remarkable how many companies, even some of the biggest and best, don't have a complaint process. They have a complaint sieve. Complaints come in, which is unavoidable, but then it's as if they leak out and go down a drain. They are not captured for analysis and tracking. Their information value is not transmitted to top-level decision makers.

After developing a good complaint measurement process, there is a second step that should be considered as a way of finding out about dissatisfied noncomplainers. Follow up with customers by telephone immediately after a transaction to get real-time feedback. Such a pro-cess is data-intensive, but it can be outsourced.

# A Painless Process for Real-Time Feedback

There is a company in Minneapolis called Service 800. In a promotional brochure the company claims to make collection of real-time feedback "a painless process by taking responsibility for drawing details of closed service orders from your problem tracking system, converting your data into a calling format, placing the calls within hours or day of the service event, and providing customized reporting of the results in paper and electronic formats."

Beware of turning this function over to untrained clerks in your office and giving them a quota of follow-up calls. The result is calls that the customer senses are hurried. It will be obvious that the caller is not really interested in what the customer thinks and feels and is simply going through the motions, checking off names on a list as fast as she or he can. Follow-up calls should cover whatever the customer wants to talk about, whether that takes thirty seconds or a half an hour. The caller needs product and service knowledge, listening skills, and empathy. The call, when properly handled, is opinion research of enor-mous potential value to the company; it should be treated accordingly.

Many companies are sitting on a wealth of information about cus-tomers but paying little attention to it. Usually that's because the information is not systematically organized and doesn't flow upward to decision makers in an easy-to-understand form. Warranties and guarantees are an example. The data from this source indicate what is unacceptable to customers and provides indications of how well the company is meeting customer expectations.

Information also flows into customer service departments. Customer service personnel can be on-line to a computer network, logging calls in a way that shows the frequency of inquiries about various product and service attributes. This information should then be made available to product developers and strategic planners.

One of the best sources of information about customers is the company's own employees who deal with customers on a day-to-day basis. To tap this information, companies can conduct surveys of customer contact personnel, carry out interviews, and organize focus groups.

## A Weakness in Self-Analysis

There is a weakness in self-analysis, though. Authors Earl Naumann and Kathleen Giel, in *Customer Satisfaction Measurement and Management*, explain:

> Typically, it is hard for us as individuals to comprehensively describe our strengths and weaknesses to someone else, especially to a friend. We are simply too close to objectively observe ourselves. One of the most difficult tasks for any artist is to paint a self-portrait.
>
> Most managers know what customers want, or at least what customers should want. After all, that is why they are managers: because of their knowledge, expertise, and skill. Collectively, the organization is much the same. The organization really should know what the customer wants. Unfortunately, those rose-colored glasses of self-analysis often paint a rosy picture, but not necessarily an accurate one.[6]

To balance the analysis of customers, it is important to have good data from outside on what customers say and do, and also to use probative techniques that get beneath the surface. In-depth interviews with customers are useful, as are focus groups in which people are brought together to express their opinions on specific issues or product attributes.

One of the most valuable, and yet least used techniques, is simply observation: methodical exposure to how your customers live and work in relation to your product or service. Seeing what people actually do in the real world often strikes sparks of creativity in trained observers that can lead to improvements and exciting new products and services.

An experienced advertising copy writer once advised an apprentice that the first step in creativity is to rise from your chair, take your hat off the rack (they wore hats in those days), and leave the office. The same advice applies to those responsible for customer satisfaction.

# References

1. Leonard A. Schlesinger and James Aeskett, "The Service-Driven Service Company," *Harvard Business Review* (September–October 1991).
2. Preface to *Command Performance* (Boston: Harvard Business Review, 1994).
3. Ibid.
4. Rick Berry, *Best's Review* (March 1995), excerpted by *Positive Impact*, Vol. 6, No. 5 (May 1995).
5. *Doors and Hardware* (February 1995).
6. Earl Naumann and Kathleen Giel, *Customer Satisfaction Measurement and Management* (Cincinnati, Ohio: Thomason Executive Press, 1995).

# Part Four

# PROGRAM SPECIFICS

Part Four deals with the basic tools that are fundamental to becoming customer centered. There are two primary reasons why companies fail to meet the test of being customer driven. The first is a lack of long-term, unrelenting commitment. The second, which is the focus of the following chapters, involves a lack of the day-to-day instrumentalities of customer satisfaction.

It is probably not possible to overstate the importance of measurement, or metrics. The number of companies that profess to be sensitive to and committed to meeting the needs and wants of customers far exceeds the number of companies employing even the most basic of customer satisfaction measurements.

There are, of course, many companies that take surveys, but this, as is shown, can be a snare and a delusion. There are also many companies urging their employees to be customer-sensitive, but failing to reward with compensation and incentives those who heed this message. Employees aren't stupid. For the most part, they will do what brings them rewards, and give short shrift to activities not considered important enough to be rewarded.

Finally, it is important for any lasting initiative to move from the front office into the culture of the workplace, a tortuous journey in many organizations. The journey must begin by recognizing the importance of the people who make and deliver products and services. The linkage between the front line and the bottom line is an important part of the understanding of what it means to make the customer the CEO.

# 18

# Measurement

W hen we think of mechanical systems that have been refined to near perfection, two examples come immediately to mind. First, the space mission that landed man on the moon was a triumph not only of human vision, determination, and courage, but also of enormously complex, intricate machines that worked flawlessly. And second, an Indy 500 car whipping around the track at a breathtaking 235 miles per hour is testimony not only to the skill and courage of the driver but to fifty years of science and technology captured in a pint-sized, shrieking machine.

These two examples have something in common not often thought of by spectators to great events. Both achievements rely heavily on telemetry, the science of indicating, measuring, recording, integrating, and transmitting data.

In the space program, virtually everything that can be measured is measured. Why? To make sure it is working right before lives are put at risk. To identify problems in time to correct them. To help analyze cause-and-effect relationships in order to design machines that perform their intended function.

The public became acquainted with telemetry when television coverage of the space program emanated from control centers with row upon row of computer screens showing the measurement of every conceivable variable of space flight. Telemetry at the Indy 500 is less well known, but there are computers in the pits providing crews with readouts on every temperature, strain, and stress that their car is undergoing while it screams its way around the track. Long before a car makes it to the Indy, every component or design idea is tested using telemetry.

Despite the proven wonders of technology, there are Indy drivers and pit crew mechanics who are disdainful of computers. They believe in relying on their *feel* for the machinery. They are like the executive who says, "Customer satisfaction measurement is a waste of money; I know what our customers want."

Another analogy can be found in medicine. Before making a diagnosis, doctors rely on many different tests. They want to know the patient's temperature, blood pressure, heart rate, symptoms, previous history, age, and weight. In many cases they want tests and analysis of body fluids, X-rays, CAT scans, and MRIs.

## The Telemetry of Business

What kind of telemetry and diagnostic tests are used in business or other organizations? The most frequently used measurements are financial: sales, profits, cash flow, return on equity, return on investment, capital spending, budgets, productivity, and, more recently, economic value added. There are a few other measuring sticks, such as market share, market penetration, and head counts.

In recent years, measurement has gone beyond the usual financial tools to include quality— things like statistical process control, scrap rates, reject rates, and performance against quality standards (such as failure rates per million units produced). However, the totality of all of these measurements falls far short of what should be measured. Most companies have taken only halting first steps on the road to *organizational telemetry*.

I've already pointed out that financial measurements, for example, are lagging indicators. They are history. When sales figures drop, it may be because of pricing decisions made months before, or product design decisions made years before, or distribution arrangements that are a decade old, or an indecipherable combination of all of these things.

Obviously sales figures are needed, but their usefulness as a diagnostic tool in making management decisions is limited. Financial measurements in general, even in the hands of those highly skilled in reading balance sheets and operating statements, are bloodless artifacts, far removed from the daily heartbeat of an organization.

## Augmenting Traditional Financial Measures

No less an authority than Professor Robert Simons of the Harvard Graduate School said: "Traditional financial indicators must be augmented by new diagnostic measures that monitor market-based variables such as quality and customer satisfaction. These nonfinancial measures, which focus attention on customers, key internal processes, and innovation, are an important step in the right direction."[1]

Simons mentions quality. There are some severe limitations here, also. Until recently, the quality movement was almost solely product-oriented, the work of engineers driving to produce products with "zero defects." Nothing wrong with that, except that studies show that customer dissatisfaction often has nothing to do with products.

Returning to our space flight analogy, measurement in most businesses is like a telemetry system that only tells you when the spaceship is about to crash, not why or how to prevent it. In Indy 500 terms, many executives believe in driving by feel rather than by fact.

What, then, should organizational telemetry include? If the customer is the CEO, it makes sense to measure everything you can that provides an inkling of what the customer thinks and feels, what the customer wants and needs now and will want and need in the future. You want to measure not only what customers say but also what they do, which is often different from what they say. And here's the rub. Customers are people. As members of the species, we all know how complex, fickle, unpredictable, ungrateful, demanding, emotional, unreasonable, unfair—and pleasant, friendly, kind, and nice—people can be. Sometimes it seems that the primary trait of the customer is sheer cussedness, and at other times being wonderful and remarkable.

It is important to recognize that the measurement tools available are, for the most part, blunt instruments. In some cases they are prone to error. In other cases, they isolate only one factor in a complex situation involving many interacting factors. Often they provide snapshots, where motion pictures are needed.

# Multiple Channels of Information Needed

To get to the truth, it is necessary to have multiple channels of information. Data from those channels should be integrated and cross-checked. Analysis and synthesis is required to transform data into information, and information into knowledge. Finally, systems are required to move the knowledge through planning and decision-making processes.

In the spacecraft control center model, data on virtually every variable that is measurable flow in from sensors. Computers compare what is happening to design parameters, and integrate the data to drive displays that can be instantly understood by human controllers. Situations requiring decisions—adjust, go, no-go—are flagged for attention or ring alarm bells. The controllers always know when and why they should be worrying on the one hand or else breaking out the champagne. There is tension, stress, and anxiety, but also a calm confidence born of knowing the facts and having the professional training to deal with them.

Contrast this with a typical corporate situation. At the quarterly review meeting, numbers are presented showing a negative deviation from plan. One of two scenarios develops. In the first, there are many different opinions of what is going wrong. Nobody knows for sure what's happening, but that doesn't diminish the vigor and authority with which opinions are expressed. Such meetings are often inconclusive because there is no agreement on the problem and consequently on a course of action. In the second scenario, a dominant personality speaks first—dogmatically. In the true tradition of groupthink, everyone else nods in agreement. This scenario often results in solutions for problems that don't exist or aren't important.

## The Dogs Won't Eat the Dog Food

In advertising circles there is a story, probably apocryphal, about a company that introduced a new dog food that didn't sell. At a stormy management meeting, the boss demanded to know why. The various minions reported defensively how they had done everything right: name selection, packaging, pricing, advertising, promotion, distribution. No one could find fault with any of those things.

In a fit of frustration, the boss exploded, "Well, dammit, why doesn't it sell?" Dead silence. Finally, a junior account executive in the back of the room stood up and with trembling voice said, "Sir, the dogs won't eat the dog food."

If you're in the dog food business, one of the first things you want to find out is whether the dogs will eat the dog food. That is a form of customer satisfaction measurement. There are many others. Depending on how terms are defined, there are at least thirty, and probably more, channels of customer satisfaction information available to organizations ( Figure 18-1).

Often data are acquired but not thought of as part of a total customer satisfaction measurement system. For example, inquiry data can be a sensitive indicator of customer interests, but they may go no further

Figure 18-1. Sources of customer satisfaction information.

---

## Customer Satisfaction Information can flow from many sources

- ❑ Surveys of customers
- ❑ Surveys of employees
- ❑ Surveys of dealers/suppliers
- ❑ Complaints
- ❑ Management contacts
- ❑ Customer service reports
- ❑ Customer visits
- ❑ Customer comment cards
- ❑ Product returns
- ❑ Warranty claims
- ❑ Focus groups
- ❑ Sales contact reports
- ❑ Engineering/design meetings with customers
- ❑ Customer advertising
- ❑ Field service reports

- ❑ Telephone activity reports
- ❑ Benchmarking
- ❑ Mystery shoppers
- ❑ Trade show intelligence
- ❑ Sales data analysis
- ❑ Lead tracking
- ❑ Customer panels
- ❑ Trade press coverage tracking
- ❑ Suggestion systems
- ❑ New product idea suggestions
- ❑ Quality performance tracking
- ❑ Customer literature, publications
- ❑ Field performance tracking

---

*Source:* Customer Inc.

than the literature fulfillment department. Complaints are really opportunities turned upside down, but they often go unreported and unanalyzed.

Sales contact reports should provide a wealth of information but often don't because sales managers are willing to accept the old wheeze that salespeople won't do reports. That may be true, but it's a problem that can be solved with training, technology, and incentives. Should it be solved? If the customer is going to be CEO, there can be no doubt.

How about management contacts with customers? Managers either are or should be in regular contact with customers. Are they trained to ask the right questions to garner customer satisfaction measurement information? Do they record and report what they learn? Does the information flow into a total customer satisfaction measurement system? Or is there a self-fulfilling belief that managers aren't any better at doing reports than salespeople?

It is paradoxical that one of the greatest obstacles to customer satisfaction measurement is one of its basic tools, the customer survey. When companies advance beyond the stage of "we know what our customers want," the first thing they think of is the annual customer survey. First of all, "annual" in the fast-paced world in which we compete is like playing one hole of golf a year and deciding that your score on that hole multiplied by 18 is your handicap. Second, surveys, while useful, are only one colored stone in a whole mosaic needed to form a complete picture of *the customer*.

Management tends to put either too much or too little faith in surveys. On the one hand, they seize on a factoid that emerges from a survey, treat it as the gospel truth, and act on it, without verification or root-cause analysis. On the other hand, they simply do not accept survey findings that appear contrary to their feel for the business.

In many organizations, even the most advanced, the acquisition of customer satisfaction information is disjointed at best. Information flow is dead-ended rather than flowing into a system. In some cases, information is suppressed. Rarely does all relevant information come together in a form that can be analyzed and synthesized. Decision makers either get too little information or more undigested data than they can cope with.

Unlike NASA controllers, who know exactly what they are seeing on their screens, the implications of it, and how to act on it, the typical person trying to understand a hodgepodge of customer satisfaction data is often more confused than enlightened. The problem is a lack of *system*, which is defined as "an orderly combination or arrangement of parts, elements, etc., into a whole, especially such combination according to some rational principle." The rational principle for a customer satisfaction measurement system is this:

> Customers decide whether we are successful. In the long run, they will decide in our favor only if they are satisfied. We can be most effective in satisfying them if we understand their wants and needs, current and future.

A successful business executive, at the end of a long career, once summed it up with this sentiment: "I finally discovered the secret of success, and it is really very simple. Find out what people want and give it to them."

Now for the orderly combination or arrangement of parts, elements, etc. (see Figure 1-1 on page 21).

# Data Input

Of the many possible sources of data, decisions are needed on which sources to employ and support. A good starting point is an assessment of existing channels of information. Figure 18-1 can be used as a checklist. Identify the channels being used. How is information collected and how often? What kind of reports are produced? Who sees them? Do data cross organizational boundaries? Are they used for decision making? How? Are there obvious gaps in the collection process? Are the efforts adequately staffed and funded?

In the spacecraft analogy, data input involves the sensors that capture information at the source, e.g., temperature, acceleration, material stress, volume, burn rates, etc. And it involves transmission and distribution of data to points where they are needed. Many companies find that they are using more channels of customer satisfaction measurement data than they realized, but they also usually find that the data flow is not tended very carefully. It is like an arrow shot in the air, ending up we know not where.

# Validation/Integration

There is a tendency in our technological society to accept numbers as facts. It is important to recognize that there are good data, bad data, and inconsequential data. For example, good data can be derived from a question on a survey, but only if the question is phrased right and the sample is scientifically selected. If those conditions do not apply, the data may be simply wrong. If there is no definition to the data, for example, if it never changes significantly, it may be inconsequential ("60 percent of the people who buy your product choose blue and 40 percent choose white, and it has been that way for years").

Two questions should be asked when validating data. Does the data collection process comply with professional research standards? Recognizing the complexity of customer satisfaction issues, are significant findings cross-checked using multiple channels of information? For example, are important survey results followed up with focus groups to explore attitudes in more depth?

After data have been validated, it is important to integrate them with data from other sources. For example, if customers say they want the lowest price but sales data show they are buying premium-priced models, there is a clear conflict that needs to be probed before product design and pricing decisions are made. It may turn out that how survey questions are being asked is flawed. It may turn out that customers perceive greater value in premium models. Perhaps packaging is making a difference, or the customers' perception of the pricing policies of the retailer where they purchase your product is a factor.

## Analysis, Synthesis, Interpretation, Extrapolation

Turning data into information and information into knowledge is one of the more difficult and challenging elements of a customer satisfaction measurement system. This may be because it seems easier than it really is.

Here is a typical scenario. A satisfaction survey reports 9.3 percent of the respondents say they are not seeing a sales representative often enough. Senior executives jump to the conclusion that there are problems in the management of the sales force. The sales manager is told to get things shaped up. Instead, these questions should be asked: Why do customers want to see a sales representative? Do they want to place orders? Are they seeking information? What kind of information? What's the most effective way to get them what they want? Is there a difference in the number of sales calls being made to the 90.7 percent of customers who are satisfied compared to the 9.3 percent who are not? Are there any common factors among the dissatisfied customers that provide clues to the root cause of dissatisfaction?

When a conclusion from data seems obvious, management should consider testing it by using a technique attributed to the Japanese; it's called "the five whys." It simply means challenging any statement by probing with *why* questions asked five times in five different ways. Here is how it works in an interchange between a researcher (R) and a customer (C):

C: I'm dissatisfied.

R: Why are you dissatisfied?

C: I had a hard time understanding the instructions that came with your product.

R: Why were they hard to understand?

C: Technical language I couldn't understand and poor illustrations.

R: Why did you decide to buy a product that needed assembly?

C: I had no choice. There were no assembled models available.

R: Why did you want this product?

C: To replace one that wore out.

R: Why did you choose our product?

C: Lowest price and assembly sounded easy.

By asking *why* five times, the researcher finds out that a dissatisfied customer has made a replacement purchase. Price is important. Product literature is not user-friendly and can be corrected with changes in language and better illustrations. Claims of easy assembly may be overstated. There may be an opportunity and competitive advantage in providing assembled products at a premium price.

There are many techniques that can be used in analysis, synthesis, interpretation, and extrapolation.

# Reporting to Functional Areas

Many organizations complain of drowning in data. In the days before downsizing and delayering, there might have been people who had the time to pore over computer printouts in search of nuggets of information that could help them in their jobs. No longer.

There are fundamental principles involved in writing memos and conducting meetings that should also be applied in communicating customer satisfaction data. State the purpose of the memo or meeting up front. Make clear the outcome or action that is expected as a result of the memo or meeting. In the case of customer satisfaction, state conclusions clearly and explain what they mean to the functional area being addressed. For example, in a report to the finance department: "Studies show clearly that customers are dissatisfied with our billing procedures. They don't believe our charges are adequately explained, and they find the format of our invoices confusing. This is a serious issue, placing us at a competitive disadvantage, and it should be corrected on a priority basis." While the issue may be complex, involving several departments and multistep procedures, the call to action should be simple and clear.

A note of caution. Because people are busy and have neither the time nor the inclination to read lengthy technical reports that require a major intellectual effort to understand, it is important to simplify and clarify—but only if the people doing the simplifying and clarifying are technically qualified and have done their homework. Conclusions should be backed by substantive research, but it is counterproductive to dump volumes of research on busy operations people.

## Decisions, Action Plans, Goals

All customer satisfaction measurement is for naught if no actions occur as a result. While this seems painfully obvious, a lack of response to customers seems more the rule than the exception. Usually it is not a matter of insensitivity or lack of good intent; it is the absence of process.

When fundamental issues are identified through customer satisfaction measurement, there should be a process that gets them placed on management's agenda for decision making. Often the issues are complex, involving trade-offs between alternatives and difficult decisions about resource allocations. There should be well thought-through processes that result in management being presented clearly defined issues, recommended solutions including organizational and budget considerations, a projection of anticipated outcomes, risk assessment, a time and action calendar for accomplishment of goals and objectives, and identification of methods to be used to monitor and measure activity. Only with these elements in place can management make sound decisions.

## Measurement of Planned Actions

One of the compelling reasons for attaching high priority to customer satisfaction measurement is that it allows you to find out whether your decisions are successful. Measurement methods that identify issues can also gauge the success of solutions to those issues. It takes the guesswork out of executive decision making.

Customer satisfaction measurement should be a closed loop of information, sensitive and self-adjusting. It should function like a thermostat controlling temperature in a building, or an autopilot flying an airplane. It should sense what matters to customers, compare that information to the goods and services provided to those customers, indicate where changes are needed, monitor the implementation of those changes, and assess their effectiveness in adjusting the overall relationship with the customer.

It is indeed simple: The key to success is to find out what the customers want and give it to them.

# Reference

1. "Forum," *CFO* (December 1994), p. 12.

# 19

# Who Is the Customer?

The simple question "Who is our customer?" can stir lively debate. The end user, some will say. Others say distributors, often referred to as the channel, are the customer. Then there are dealers. A case can be made for decision influencers. Retailers can be important; people who sell your product are also customers, in a sense.

The debate usually is to try to identify *the* customer to be targeted by marketing and sales. When trying to identify *the* customer, arguments revolve around who plays the biggest role in the purchase decision. Who's the big kahuna? The same question arises when you are thinking about listening to the voice of the customer. Which customer? Listen to the wrong "customer" and what you hear may be irrelevant. Put too heavy a weight on attitudes among one sector of influencers while ignoring another, and the resulting decisions can be disastrously misguided.

From an analytical point of view, it would be desirable to weigh the influence of all of the people who affect your distribution chain. It would be nice if you knew for sure that end-user preferences affected sales by $X$ percent while the decisions of purchasing agents had effect $Y$. Unfortunately, that degree of precision is unattainable, at least for now.

## Common Sense Dictates Whose Opinions Matter Most

You can apply customer satisfaction measurement techniques and technology to all of the links in your distribution chain. Where discrepancies exist, common sense usually dictates whose opinions matter the most. For example, end users may be very price conscious, but they never even have a choice if the retailer, who is margin conscious, decides not to give shelf position to the product because he or she can't make money on it.

When thinking about which "customers" to pay attention to, the wisest choice is to cast the net broadly. They are *all* important—*they* being anyone who has an influence in whether you are perceived as satisfying your customers. Obviously this influences the design of a customer satisfaction measurement system.

The subtlety of all of this is illustrated by the remarkable success of Packard Bell Electronics, which began in obscurity a decade ago and now sells more personal computers in the United States than anyone else—more than colossus IBM, or Compaq, or Apple (which started it all). How could this happen?

First of all, it is not exactly a secret that consumers are brand conscious. With this in mind, Israeli-born entrepreneur Beny Alagem bought the name Packard Bell from a defunct consumer electronics company. It had obvious appeal, smacking as it does of Hewlett-Packard and the Bell System. Next Alagem chose a counterintuitive strategy for his new PC company. Let the big guys continue to sell to big corporations. Cater instead to consumers who shop at the big, killer outlets—Best Buy, Circuit City, Wal-Mart, Sears. Work closely with the department stores and consumer electronics dealers, helping them learn how to satisfy computer customers.

While all this was going on, IBM and Compaq continued to pursue their corporate strategies, heads down, looking neither left nor right. To them, consumer retailers were an "alternate channel" that didn't even show up when you rounded sales numbers.

Alagem was quoted in *Fortune* as saying, "The vision of the company is to listen to what the consumer wants and to provide an innovative product with the latest technology—to become the voice of the people when it comes to the PC."[1] Saccharine, to be sure, but read on.

How do they listen to the voice of the people? First they developed a warm, partnering relationship with retailers and their staffs. They get more than just shelf space as a result; they get early word from the sales floor on what people are saying and asking for. When customers said they wanted PCs equipped with CD-ROMs and built-in stereo speakers for multimedia, the company quickly brought out a whole new line that was so equipped. Sales took off, leaving Compaq and IBM eating Packard Bell's dust again.

How does an upstart like Packard Bell get cozy with the likes of

Wal-Mart, Sears, Circuit City, and Best Buy? Simple. They find out what they want and give it to them. There are all the usual things: price, delivery, quality, responsiveness, product variety, co-op ad dollars, liberal return policy. But there's even more. The home electronics people at Sears had not been very successful in selling PCs when Packard Bell showed up in 1989. Packard Bell created in-store displays and demonstrations especially for Sears and helped train Sears salespeople. Sears' computer sales have tripled since then. Chuck Cebuhar, head of Sears' home electronics division, told *Fortune*, "Partnership is one of the most misused words in business, but Packard Bell is a great partner. They are as good and responsive as you can get."[2] In 1994, Sears gave Packard Bell its Product Development Source of the Year award. Wal-Mart and Staples have given Packard Bell similar awards.

If a customer wanders in and asks a Sears salesperson which computer is the best deal, what would you guess the answer is likely to be?

In paying close attention to four "customers," that is, end users, retail executives, retail sales staff, and Packard Bell's own employees, note what the company has done:

- They have chosen a customer satisfaction strategy and determined to become the best in the industry at it. The strategy is to be the preeminent marketer of PCs through mass retailers of consumer electronics. Everyone in the company understands the strategy and supports it.
- They listen intently to the end user in this fickle, fast-moving market and respond immediately with the latest technology, the greatest variety, and the most attractive perceived value.
- They know that retailers are the keystone of their success, so they treat them as valued partners and friends.
- They know that none of this is possible without a spirited and committed workforce supporting and backing up every strategic move that is made. They work hard at things like vision, spirit, and focus, and according to industry observers they have succeeded in getting rank-and-file loyalty.

In many industries, there is schizophrenia about who the customer is. The auto industry is a classic. From the time Henry Ford decided all cars should be black (because black paint was cheaper) right up until the Japanese conquest of the market in the 1980s, the industry behaved as though the end user was essentially irrelevant and dealers were the enemy. If this assertion seems too harsh, consider the old mentality in Detroit: The auto companies would decide what was best for the public, and the public would buy it. They always had. As for the dealers, that benighted bunch of scoundrels needed to be managed and controlled lest they get too uppity. Design decisions were made in the rarefied air of the design studios. Relationships between dealers and the factory could best be described as a running gun battle.

For the most part, these paradigms of the auto industry have changed, but the change has not come easily. When the Japanese car-makers showed the American public what quality could be and American buyers responded by abandoning the industry's big three in droves, Detroit learned a painful lesson about customer satisfaction. It became apparent that the public was fed up with the sales shenanigans and lousy service of the stereotypical auto dealer. It also became apparent that a truce between factory and dealer was necessary if they were to work together to find ways to respond to customer expectations.

Out of this turmoil came the Customer Satisfaction Index (CSI), which is used extensively in the auto industry. Buy any car now, and you are likely to receive a survey in the mail questioning you about your satisfaction with the entire purchase-and-service relationship. The factories crunch these survey numbers and provide feedback to the dealers. A dealer's interest in the CSI is more than academic. Score above a certain level, compared to other dealers in the area, and the factory pays incentives for every car sold during that measurement period. Score too low, and the factory is all over you like a cheap suit. Many dealers provide incentives for their salespeople based on how well the dealership is doing on its CSI.

The CSI has been a source of some tension between factory and dealer because of the propensity of the factory to use the numbers punitively, and because of disagreements over the wording of questions on the surveys. But then, harmony between factory and dealer is a new concept. In 1990 Dallas Cadillac dealer Carl Sewell wrote a book entitled *Customers for Life: How to Turn That One-Time Buyer Into a Lifetime Customer.* He unwittingly makes an astonishing revelation about the state of affairs between dealer and factory:

"No one is closer to the customer than the retailer. That's why it's important for them (the factory) to listen to you. Cadillac's General Manager, John Grettenberger, decided when he got the job five years ago that he wanted to have dealers involved in the product development process.

"So John put a group of us—dealers, engineers, manufacturing guys, and designers—in a room, and he kept us there for three days.

What Cadillac got, for the first time, was a useful exchange of views and information."[3]

Duh!

That would have been in 1985, if Sewell's book is interpreted accurately on when the meeting took place. Note that he said this "useful exchange of views and information" was occurring "for the first time." Is it possible that a luxury-car maker, part of a company of which it once was said "What's good for General Motors is good for the nation," first got around to a useful exchange of views with its dealers in 1985? Yes, it is.

This is not dumping on the auto industry. Similar examples of disconnects between companies and the influencers who hold their fate in their hands can be found in most industries. It's a result of the inward-looking culture of most organizations.

## No One Is Closer to the Customer Than the Retailer

Sewell makes a good point, that no one is closer to the customer than the retailer. Put another way, the sales organization, whether it be a direct sales force, reps, dealers, or telemarketers, is on the firing line with the customer. How often are these people treated as customers themselves?

If a customer is defined as anybody who influences a sale, these frontline workers are definitely customers. Their degree of satisfaction can profoundly influence the degree of success enjoyed by their employer. There are damaging stereotypes about salespeople that are corrosive in the organizations where they exist. For example: salespeople are viewed as glad-handers more interested in protecting their turf and piling up easy commissions than in doing the groundwork to get new accounts. They are lazy, irresponsible, lax in producing reports, and not to be trusted. They are not businesspeople; they don't understand the big picture. If it weren't for quotas, incentives, and pressure from the home office, they would never get the job done. What they really need is a good whap up the side of the head every now and then.

If there is anything worse than a direct sales force, it is reps. They're an ungrateful lot who don't really do any selling (the stereotype runs); they just write orders. The "independent" part of their name is accurate. They are too independent. Half the time they won't do what the manufacturer wants them to do because that's too much like work for an established rep (the stereotype continues). There is a dark suspicion that most of their time is spent on somebody else's line. They are all too willing to cancel an agreement and respond to the siren call of a competitor. But if you cancel them, you're likely to get sued.

Distributors—so goes yet another notion—are a necessary evil. They don't *sell* anything, they just wait for orders. They're always playing off one manufacturer against another. Their business systems are archaic, and they are tiresomely slow to make improvements. They are unwilling to stock enough product, and unreceptive to new and unproven products. They're always complaining about something or making unreasonable demands on the factory.

These stereotypes, while they have some basis in truth, become dangerous as self-fulfilling prophecies. When people are treated negatively, they behave negatively. It is uncanny the way people behave in the manner expected of them! You think I'm a jerk, I'll show you how big a jerk I am. The opposite is also true: High expectations bring out the best in people.

## Salespeople Are Prime Customers

The lesson to be learned from this is not obscure, although it is manifestly ignored across a broad spectrum of business. Salespeople (whatever their title or relationship to the company) are prime customers. They can't be expected to do a good job of satisfying their customers if they are not satisfied themselves. What does it take to satisfy them? Treat them as customers, partners, full-fledged members of the team whose thoughts and opinions matter. Keep them fully informed. Ask them what they think. Respond to them. Recognize them for their ability to satisfy their customers. Most of all, recognize and honor the truth of what Sewell wrote: "No one is closer to the customer."

There is another customer who usually gets slighted: the internal customer. The work product of everyone in every organization is done for somebody else. It's like a bucket brigade, with sloshing buckets of water being passed from hand to hand. Only a small percentage of employees in most organizations work on the front line, where the product or service is handed off to the outside, either to end users or to a link in the distribution chain—where the water gets poured on the flames.

The majority of people hand their work off to fellow workers: engineering to production, the cook to the wait staff, word processing to secretarial, production to shipping. Out of this was born the concept of the internal customer. Everyone can be considered as working for customers, and everyone is a customer of someone else. A nifty idea in theory, but what about the reality? External customers can show their displeasure by going somewhere else; the internal customer doesn't usually have that option. It is clear that the external customer ultimately pays the bills: It is not clear that some guy in another department has much effect on the economics of the business.

For the concept of the internal customer to work effectively, several things have to happen:

- In most organizations the necessary starting point is recognition of the need for cultural change, which requires definition of the vision, communication, training . . . and patience over an extended period of time.
- Insofar as possible, the internal customer has to be given the same kind of power that the external customer enjoys: the option of seeking an alternative supplier, the ability to complain without fearing it will backfire, recognition as being a customer who deserves respect and attention.
- How the internal customer relationships are functioning should be measured using the same tools as are used in external customer satisfaction measurement: surveys, focus groups, complaints, suggestions, and operational data such as on-time delivery, prompt answering of telephones, and quality of work performed.
- There should be rewards and recognition for good performance, and a continuous improvement effort to root out deficiencies.

It is important to recognize that there are many obstacles in the way of the internal customer idea. Usually it is a mistake to talk about it if the company is not willing to make the fundamental changes needed to bring it into reality. To talk it and not walk it is to breed discord and cynicism.

In our society, people grow up learning to mind their own business, keep their own counsel. They are taught not to squeal, tattle, complain, or make waves. Deviate from the go-along norm and you are shunned, in some cases punished. Don't tell the teacher, don't tell the boss. It is the gang or cult that comes first, not the individual. The code of silence must be observed, revered. Slit the wrists and press them together in a pledge of solidarity.

These cultural norms fly in the face of the internal customer idea.

They are deeply rooted and can be changed only with time and persistence.

One large company found this out in an interesting way. The CEO was concerned about the lack of African Americans in the executive ranks. To get some advice on the problem of executive diversity, he had breakfast with a small group of black executives who had succeeded in getting into management positions. He got more than he bargained for. The blacks leveled with him to a degree he was unaccustomed to, on a whole range of subjects concerning the necessity to change the culture of the company. He found their candor so valuable that he continued to meet with the group, unofficially and quietly, for years as he worked to transform the culture of the company.

One of the members of that group explained that African Americans are more inclined than their Caucasian brethren to face up to reality, to tell it like it is. At least that was his opinion. He saw it as a natural sociological response to centuries of repression. How do you get people to accept the idea that their fellow workers are encouraged to be critical of their work? How do you get them to go to extremes to meet deadlines imposed by another department? How do you get them to maintain a cheerful demeanor in the face of unreasonable demands by peers who work for the same company they do?

## Understanding and Alignment Are the Beginning

It has to begin with understanding and alignment. Everyone must understand and accept the idea that their ultimate success—in fact their survival—depends on the satisfaction of the ultimate customer, and this in turn depends on the satisfaction of all of the customers in the bucket brigade, any one of whom can spill the water before it reaches the flames.

One of the oddities of corporate life is the prevailing idea that the CEO can make things happen with a speech or two, and then get on with whatever that particular CEO perceives the *real* work to be. When Harry Truman was thinking about turning over the Oval Office to Dwight Eisenhower, he commented that Eisenhower was in for a shock. As a general used to having his orders followed, Eisenhower would learn that presidential orders can be hopelessly impotent.

Make no mistake, there is a lot of work involved for organizations that want to be effective in creating an environment where internal customer satisfaction flourishes.

# References

1. Alison L. Sprout, "Packard Bell," *Fortune* (June 12, 1995), p. 82.
2. Ibid., p. 84.
3. Carl Sewell, *Customers for Life: How to Turn That One-Time Buyer Into a Lifetime Customer* (New York: Simon & Schuster, 1990), p. 136.

# 20

# Surveys

To understand the power of opinion research surveys, you need only listen to political analysts in advance of an election. The ability to forecast election results has become almost uncanny. On the other hand, for an inkling of how misunderstood and misused surveys can be, you need only sample how they are used in business in connection with customer satisfaction measurement.

Businesspeople seem to think taking a survey is a no-brainer. Interpreting the results, they appear to believe, is an exercise in the obvious, as though someone with no medical training could determine the state of their health by taking their own temperature and blood pressure. There are some areas of business where everyone seems to feel competent to pitch in their two cents' worth. Advertising copy is one, and surveys are another. Executives who usually won't make a move without lawyers and accountants at their side think nothing of writing ad copy or deciding what questions to ask on a survey. The root cause of the problem is that advertising and surveys appear deceptively simple, and familiar. Everybody knows what ads look like; everybody has filled out a survey.

In the customer satisfaction field, the consequences of amateurism can be serious. There is a propensity to waste time and money. But even worse, misleading information can result in strategic missteps. A failure to obtain data suited to action can handicap the decision making process. And pseudoindications of satisfied customers can lull companies into dangerous complacency.

# Common Mistakes in Surveys

In regard to surveys, there is a long and tortuous list of mistakes and miscalculations made every day by organizations. There seems to be little discrimination among the miscreants; the same mistakes are made by the prosperous giant companies and by small entrepreneurial ventures. Here are some of the most common.

## Mistaking a Blunt Instrument for a Scalpel

Even the best surveys provide only crude data that need to be cross-checked against other research sources for validation and probed for meaning using other techniques. Okay, 82.5 percent of the respondents to your survey are either very satisfied or satisfied with your company. So what? It doesn't mean much unless you also find out: Why? Is that a good score, or a bad score? What factors could change it? How does it compare with the competitors? Snapshots are fine, but what's the trend? What is influencing it? Which factors influence satisfaction most in the minds of customers?

## Mabel Can Do It

You know Mabel. She's the workhorse who will take on anything. "If you want something done, give it to a busy person" is her philosophy. No matter that Mabel has no professional training in surveys or research of any kind. She can read a book or take a course. And she's a tiger for getting things done. She'll talk to everybody who needs to be involved.

## It'll Be Cheaper If We Do It

Wrong. It is usually much more expensive than going outside, if you calculate all of the costs completely: salaries of the people involved, overhead, out-of-pocket expense, learning-curve expenses, amateur mistakes requiring rework, and absence of the economies of scale that favor the people who do surveys every day.

## The Christmas Tree Model

Lots of people have questions they would like included in a survey. Tolerating this results in a survey that is like a Christmas tree, with ornaments hanging all over it. Ancillary questions clog up the arteries of surveys, reducing the number of respondents who take the time to fill out the questionnaire and complicating the task of interpreting results.

## To Survey or Not to Survey, That Is the Question

In many cases, a survey is the least effective way to find out what you want to know. Focus groups or open-ended interviews often are better ways to zero in on what you should be measuring. Knee-jerk decisions to conduct surveys whenever questions arise can result in survey overload for customers.

## The Allure of "Annual"

It is as though an immutable natural cycle must be obeyed. The idea of an annual survey fits nicely with conventional budget planning, but it probably has nothing to do with useful research. An annual survey is a snapshot that ages quickly, whereas what is usually needed is fresh trend data to guide real-time activity.

## The Dreaded Useless Question

Product-oriented marketing people have a tendency to ask questions about things that are irrelevant to customers. Every question on a survey should be challenged by asking of the survey makers, "What do we do with this information once we have it?" If the answer to that challenge is not convincing, the question should be dropped.

## A Jumble of Jargon

Every industry has terminology that is familiar to people in the industry but as mysterious as a foreign language to the uninitiated. These terms tend to creep into questionnaires. The computer biz, for example, is awash in nerdspeak. The result is that customers are either turned off and don't respond, or they answer without really understanding the question, producing spurious survey results.

## Is There a Question Here?

Amateurs regularly fall into the trap of the compound question. "Do you or the people in your company frequently use overnight package delivery services?" The respondent is left to puzzle over what is really being asked. Who are we talking about here? What does *frequently* mean? Are we talking about "packages" meaning products, or are documents and letters included? The answers that come back are likely to be as impenetrable as the question.

## Is the Purpose Measurement or Research?

There is a difference between measurement and research. Mail surveys, by and large, are measurement tools. There is little likelihood that they will uncover elements of customer thinking and attitudes different from the preconceived notions that underlie the questions; the questions are contaminated by the attitudes of the people who compose them. People respond to questions the way they are asked. Even open-ended questions tend to draw responses within a framework that has been established by the questionnaire. By way of contrast, research should be scrupulously neutral in a quest for unvarnished fact and opinion. Its tools are likely to be observation, the study of behavior, analysis of facts, and experimentation.

## Statistical Reliability

How many questionnaires should you send out to get enough back to have statistically reliable results? The answer is that there is no answer until you deal with an array of technical questions. How accurate do the results have to be to serve your purpose? How big is your universe? How complete is your database? What kind of information are you looking for? Are you employing the methods that the pros use to get high response rates?

## Ready, Fire, Aim

In their haste to get a project completed, many organizations compile questionnaires and fire them off into an unsuspecting world without any pretesting. Companies that wouldn't think about introducing a new product without beta testing it go blithely forward with a survey that has not been exposed to the public. Pretesting is needed to determine whether people understand the questions, and whether the responses produce statistical differentials that are meaningful and useful. Just as every writer needs an editor, every questionnaire needs criticism, in advance.

For many executives, the subject of customer satisfaction measurement begins and ends with an occasional home-grown survey. Anyone who reads this book cannot escape the message that there is a lot more to it than that, but it is also important to understand that the survey subject alone is more complex than it might appear at first. Karl Albrecht, a columnist for *Quality Digest* magazine, writes:

> Surveying is rapidly gaining in popularity as a management tool. It's time we brought some skill and discipline to the process, stopped wasting time and money, and stopped confusing ourselves and other people. No one should be allowed to send surveys to customers, clients, prospects, employees, or anyone whose views are important to the organization's success without having at least some basic training in survey methods.
>
> It doesn't take a statistical genius, but it does take some practical knowledge and common sense. Surveys can be tremendously valuable, but only if they measure something worth measuring.[1]

Here is a checklist of questions that should be asked by any executive considering approving a survey project:

- [ ] Is this the best way to get the answers we are looking for?
- [ ] Do we know what we are going to do with the information when we get it?
- [ ] Are we planning to do surveys often enough to give us the kind of trend data we need?
- [ ] Do we have the processes in place to validate and cross-check the information we expect from the survey?
- [ ] Have we been thorough in comparing the merits of outsourcing versus doing it inside?
- [ ] Do we know when it is best to do surveying by mail and when by telephone?
- [ ] Are we planning to pretest questionnaires?
- [ ] Are we working with accurate, up-to-date mailing lists?
- [ ] Do we have the discipline to keep survey questionnaires down to twenty or fewer questions?
- [ ] Is our focus on what is important to customers, not just to our product marketing people?
- [ ] Do we know how to reduce sample size and cut costs by getting a 60–70 percent return rate on mailed surveys?

People are astonished to hear that it is possible to get response rates in that 60–70 percent range. The Readex company in St. Paul, Minnesota, which does in excess of four hundred mail surveys a year for clients, routinely gets response rates in that range. There are a number of factors involved. Readex sends out alert letters in advance, notifying people that they will be receiving an important survey. All correspondence is handled in a professional, highly personal manner. Envelopes are individually addressed and sent with postage stamps, not metered. People who don't respond in a reasonable time are sent a second invitation to do so. Usually there is an incentive for responding, such as a dollar bill folded over the letter. Questionnaires are in booklet form and appear to be easy to complete quickly.

The various techniques that can be used in mail surveys to increase response rates have been tested and proven over time. Each of the little subtleties or niceties, such as using stamps rather than metering, makes a difference. Response rates at the high end of the scale require using *all* of the tricks of the trade. A high response rate is worth the effort when you consider the benefits. Statistically representative results can be achieved with a smaller mailing, which reduces costs and minimizes survey overload.

# It Is Up to the Client to Decide the Best Approach

Vendors who specialize in either mail surveys or telephone surveys tend, not unexpectedly, to be advocates for their particular methodology. It is up to the client to weigh the differences and decide on the best approach.

Mail surveys are good for identifying overall attitudes. How are we doing? How important are various attributes of product or service? How are we doing compared with our competition? However, understanding why customers have developed particular attitudes—the causal factors—can usually be probed more effectively in a telephone interview in which *why* questions are more easily asked. Mail surveys also tend to be less expensive per respondent, but there is a trade-off with regard to immediacy. The entire mail survey process takes weeks, even months. Telephone surveys can be accomplished and the results reported within hours after a transaction has occurred, while the experience is fresh in the mind of the respondent.

An increasingly popular way to calculate and report customer satisfaction data is an index. The Customer Satisfaction Index (CSI) is a technique for lumping together a group of attributes, weighting them according to perceived importance, and then calculating an overall satisfaction number that takes on added meaning when compared to others providing the same products or services.

The most familiar example is the auto industry, where the manufacturers survey customers on their experience in purchasing a new or used car or having their vehicle serviced. Each dealership gets a monthly report with a CSI number; it is a composite of numerical rankings on how well the dealership is doing on various attributes of product and service compared to national averages and dealerships in the same geographical area.

A pharmaceutical company, which has laboratories that perform tests for hospitals and clinics, conducts surveys of their customers—doctors, nurses, and administrators—on their satisfaction with the company's labs and those of competitors. There are questions about response time, courtesy, accuracy, billing, and other factors. Lab managers use the data to focus on areas needing improvement, and the CSI is used by management to rate the performance of lab personnel.

The most difficult challenge in creating a CSI is deciding which attributes to measure and then weighting them according to their importance in the overall scheme of things. It is not uncommon at the start of the process to come up with a list of fifty or sixty attributes that are candidates for inclusion in the index. A list of attributes can be compiled by conducting interviews with customers, asking them what they consider to be important in their relationship with the company, and interviewing people at all levels in the organization to get their answers to the same questions. Attributes tend to fall into groupings, making it possible to winnow a list of up to sixty attributes down to a dozen or so factors. Skillfully written survey questions can elicit customer responses that accurately reflect attitudes about a factor representing a group of attributes.

It is important to keep the number of factors under twenty. Any more than that and the survey questionnaire becomes unwieldy, response rates drop, and it becomes very difficult to analyze the results. IBM, which started out with a one-hundred-question survey form, has reduced it to fewer than twenty. The auto industry has struggled to respond to criticism by putting its CSI surveys on a diet (see Appendix F).

When it comes to weighting factors in a CSI—what percentage of the total each should represent—the focus should be entirely on what the customers think. That may be at odds with the internal view of people working in marketing, sales, product development, customer service, or operations. A bias in favor of the customer point of view reflects the purpose of the whole process which, after all, is customer satisfaction measurement.

## An Index Can Be a Valuable Tool

The beauty of a CSI is that it is a kind of stake in the ground. With a number determined periodically, using precisely the same measurement methodology, movement in one direction or the other is apparent. It is a valuable tool for any organization. The value is enhanced if the data cover multiple units of an organization and are compounded once again whenever an entire industry is covered.

## Reference

1. Karl Albrecht, "The Use and Misuse of Surveys," *Quality Digest* (November 1994), pp. 21-22.

# *21*

# Compensation

The debate goes on, as it has for decades. How do you motivate employees? But with the advent of customer satisfaction measurement, the debate has taken a new turn, with a new question: Should incentive compensation be tied to customer satisfaction measurement? The direct answer is "Yes, but."

First, incentive compensation *does* work, despite the protestations of those who argue that money ranks fairly low whenever you ask people to classify the things that are important to them in their jobs. The factors that lead to job satisfaction tend to be achievement, recognition, responsibility, and advancement, according to psychologists who study the subject. However, it is important to recognize that money is a complex, emotion-laden subject. In its most basic sense, it provides a living. It can also serve as a score-keeping device and as a way to grant especially meaningful recognition. For many it represents prestige, comfort, luxury, and security, each a powerful drive in its own right. Money symbolizes achievement, recognition, responsibility, and advancement, and so it must be regarded as more than just cash.

## Financial Incentives Work

When you strip away the psychobabble, the plain fact is that financial incentives work. It doesn't require a behaviorist to point out, or studies to prove, that in dealing with employees, what you motivate with money is what you get.

There are the old-school hard-liners who are opposed to incentives in general. They insist that you do what we tell you and we'll pay you what we agreed on; that's it. The incentive (they add with a scowl) is that if you work hard you get to keep your job.

This attitude harkens back to the era of "KITA." Nearly three decades ago, psychologist Frederick Herzberg achieved his fifteen minutes of fame by, among other things, coining the term, which was delicately described as a kick in the pants. Herzberg's point, incidentally, was that KITA doesn't work. What works, he contended, was giving employees challenging work in which they can assume responsibility.

The argument against incentives is that after a while they become entitlements, losing their power to motivate. That's true when they are not thought through carefully, based on fair measurement, and legitimately earned. Like any other management tool, they serve a purpose when properly used, but a hammer cannot be used to saw boards. To cavalierly reject incentives because they have the potential for misuse is to deny yourself a powerful tool that can help keep people focused, enthusiastic, and productive.

Returning to the question, how do you motivate workers? You don't, at least not for long. They motivate themselves. What are the generators of self-motivation? For starters, there are such things as pressure and anxiety. In the physical world, nothing much happens without the presence of friction; a vehicle can neither accelerate nor stop without it.

# Productivity Suffers When Uncertainty Is High

Psychologist and consultant Judith M. Bardwick says:

> We psychologists have long been concerned with the debilitating effects of too much anxiety and we know that productivity suffers when uncertainty is high. But we've failed to realize the equally destructive effects of too little anxiety.
>
> People are not at their keenest when life is too safe. When people receive without having to achieve they are protected from failure. There's no punishment for not achieving. At first glance that may seem like a good thing, but it is not. By protecting people from risk, we destroy their self-esteem. We rob them of the opportunity to become strong, competent people.
>
> Facing risk is the only way we gain confidence, because confidence is the result of mastering challenge. Confidence is an internal state. It cannot be given; it can only be earned. The only way to

get genuinely confident is to be familiar with fear and then conquer it.[1]

Bardwick summarizes her views this way: "In the short run, requiring that people earn what they receive is vastly harsher than simply giving it to them. But in the long run, it is the only way that people can gain self-esteem and independence."[2]

Incentives provide an intelligent way to meter out anxiety and require people to earn what they receive. The result is self-confidence, self-esteem, independence—the generators of self-motivation. Bardwick mentions fear. Isn't that a bad thing in the workplace? Deming certainly said it was, insisting that it should be "driven out." The strange thing about fear is that as paralyzing as it may be, it loses its sting. When people's fears are realized (they get fired, divorced, rejected), they find out they can live through it. Acceptance sets in, and fear loses its power.

Moderate levels of pressure and anxiety are sustainable and can be positive, exciting, and exhilarating. It is what keeps marathoners running, sky divers diving, and mountain climbers climbing. It also applies to the less adventurous among us in the workplace. Put yourself in this situation. You work for an organization whose dominant value is customer satisfaction. It is clear to everyone that they are involved in satisfying internal/external customers. There are comprehensive systems for measuring customer satisfaction, with quantitative results posted for everyone to see. Your supervisor calls you in and says, "From now on, 40 percent of your pay is going to be based on how well you do with regard to customer satisfaction. If we do as well as we are doing now, your pay will be about the same as it is now. If performance drops, so will your paycheck. If we do better, you'll make more money."

Welcome to the world of anxiety and pressure! Your initial reaction depends on whether you are basically an optimist or pessimist. The optimist says, "Great, a chance to make more money, maybe even what I'm worth." The pessimist says, "Just what I thought: Management has found a new way to cut our pay, and make us work harder to boot."

In this scenario, both optimists and pessimists have questions:

- How much more or less am I likely to make?
- Are the measurement systems credible and fair?
- How much effect can I really have on the measurements that determine my pay?

- Will I be penalized for the actions of some of the goof-offs I work with?
- Is management going to take the same medicine they are prescribing for us?
- Is this going to last, or is it just another program *du jour*?
- Are we going to get the equipment and support we need to do the job right?

These questions indicate the complexity of installing customer-satisfaction-based incentive compensation programs. Is it worth the effort? Each company has to determine that for itself. IBM Rochester did. They calculated that a one-point increase in their customer satisfaction index was worth $250 million in new business.

It should be evident from the questions raised in the scenario that there are basic issues to be addressed before installing incentive compensation programs linked to customer satisfaction. They include:

- Establishment of a corporate culture built on customer satisfaction as a basic value
- Creation of customer satisfaction measurement systems and processes that produce reliable results
- Awareness, on the part of everyone in the company, of the direct and personal effect they have on customer satisfaction, whether fellow employees or end users
- Clarity of management's long-term commitment to customer satisfaction as a strategic driving force
- A commitment to involve everyone in a collaborative process necessary to devise compensation systems that will be accepted as fair
- Recognizing that what is good for the goose is good for the gander; make sure executive compensation is also linked rigorously to customer satisfaction

Linking customer satisfaction measurement and compensation is a favorite subject at seminars and workshops, but not many organizations have achieved it in a meaningful way. Why? Well, for one reason, it's hard to do it right. It is much easier to buy into some simplistic blanket compensation program.

Management by objective (MBO) programs were supposed to pay executives based on how well they achieved quantifiable objectives worked out in concert with their bosses. In many companies, MBO became a transparent sham. Bosses still found ways to reward the sycophants and treat those less favored routinely. Goals often were arbitrary and capricious. The paperwork was a pain. Discussions between bosses and those working for them were perfunctory at best. In time, MBO died a deserved death.

The term *pay for performance* has had an appealing ring to it for years. It is supposed to alert people to the idea that if they perform well, they will be paid accordingly. The problem is that most people get standard raises, falling somewhere in a range based on cost of living, the economy, and how well the company is doing overall. Employees are not oblivious; talk of pay for performance gets ignored with a shrug.

## The Problems With Profit Sharing

The answer, some companies think, is profit sharing. Profit sharing is a simple idea, in fact too simple to be very effective at the individual level.

The problem with the profit sharing concept is that it is remote from the daily lives of workers. Because it is remote, it is unlikely to have much effect on attitudes, actions, and decision making day in and day out—in other words, the arena in which customer satisfaction or dissatisfaction occurs.

A too-simplistic, one-size-fits-all approach to incentive compensation is typical of the kind of thinking that goes on in too many human resource or personnel departments. Think about the Christmas bonus, standard fare in many companies. It may give management a warm feeling, like reading *A Christmas Carol*, but as a once-a-year event it is irrelevant for at least eleven and one-half months of the year. Many recipients are either disappointed or angry, thinking it should be bigger. Those are certainly wonderful emotions to arouse—and at considerable expense to the company. Once the giving of Christmas bonuses has been established, management dares not discontinue the practice. It therefore fits the classic definition of an entitlement. Announcing the Christmas bonus or passing out checks is to many executives a patronizing task they hate. So why do companies keep doing it? Tradition, inertia, fear of change, apprehension about the consequences of cutting it out . . . who knows?

## The Untidy Mess of Failed Bonus Programs

An opportunity to clean up the untidy mess of failed bonus programs and other compensation anachronisms exists when sound programs of incentive compensation based on customer satisfaction measurement are being developed and introduced. For leaders who have the courage of their convictions, an out-with-the-old, in-with-the-new approach to compensation makes good sense and is likely to be received with enthusiasm.

If there ever was a company steeped in entitlements, it was IBM. One of their managers recalls that at a time of companywide belt-tightening a technician earning nearly $90,000 a year took advantage of an open-door policy and went to a senior executive with a complaint about getting a raise of 6 percent. The technician protested that he was entitled to 11 percent because that was what he was used to getting. That was the old IBM. Now the company is experimenting with serious linkages between customer satisfaction and compensation. In some divisions, account managers have 40 percent of their compensation determined by how well they are rated by their customers, based on scrupulously independent customer satisfaction surveys.

Taco Bell store managers, and all of the employees under them, earn incentive compensation in proportion to how well their unit does on a customer satisfaction index computed on the basis of surveys of customers. Many auto dealers pass out monthly bonuses to sales and service personnel in direct proportion to factory-conducted customer satisfaction survey results.

As with all such systems, cunning employees figure out ways to diddle the results to their own advantage, and safeguards must be built into the system to prevent that from occurring. Employees have been known to plead with their customers to give them a good score on a survey because it affects their pay. One such horror story influenced the thinking of an executive of a large retail operation. He had been thinking about bonuses linked to customer satisfaction until he went on a vacation cruise. His steward for the cruise gave him a sob story about how important it was for him to get a good customer satisfaction rating so he could support his family. The executive found it a turnoff and was concerned about this kind of thing happening to customers of his stores.

There are, of course, a couple of ways to prevent abuse. Make clear to employees that they are, under no circumstances, to even mention customer satisfaction ratings to the customers they deal with, and that any infractions will be penalized. A question can be added to a survey: "Has any employee of this company attempted to influence your responses to these questions unfairly?" If the answer is yes, the survey is rejected as invalid. There are other preventive safeguards. If an employee consistently performs much better than peers on customer satisfaction measurements, telephone calls can be made to customers to spot-check whether what they say is consistent with findings derived by other means.

Linking customer satisfaction data and compensation was described by Naumann and Giel as "an extremely important change that reinforces a shift to customer-driven continuous improvement." They went on to say: "This is very new for virtually all businesses. The changes involve modifying an organization's reward systems to include customer-driven elements. By linking rewards to CSM data, an organization sends a powerful message to all employees. That message is that customer satisfaction is so important that it must involve *everyone*. By rewarding employees for improvements in customer satisfaction, an organization is reinforcing all of the other change efforts."[2]

Because it's difficult to build an equitable system, get the ideas and help of the people who are directly involved. Each employee should be asked how he or she feels performance against customer satisfaction goals should be measured—what does the employee think would be fair? This helps make the customer satisfaction vision come alive as real, imminent, and understandable.

When each individual understands how measurements are going to be taken and how they bear directly on compensation, the posted charts and graphs of measurement data get exciting. There is something inherent in human makeup that responds very positively to keeping score. It feeds self-motivation. Everyone wants to see the team do better, the curves go up, the percentages get higher. But with anything as complex as converting customer satisfaction numbers into dollars and cents on a paycheck, inevitably there are arguments about what is fair and what isn't, what people individually can influence and what they can't. After differing points of view and ideas have been expressed—some contradictory, some absurd, some self-serving—management must step in and make final decisions.

If the process is carried out with patience and understanding, most employees accept the results and get on with the program enthusiastically. If the end result is perceived as fair, even the holdouts eventually become converts.

# Reference

1. Judith Bardwick, *Danger in the Comfort Zone* (New York: AMACOM, 1991), p. 32.
2. Earl Naumann and Kathleen Giel, *Customer Satisfaction Measurement and Management* (Cincinnati, Ohio: Thomason Executive Press, 1995).

# 22

# Production/ Operations

A review of the literature on customer satisfaction reveals an unfortunate omission. Little is written about the role of the people who actually make and deliver products: the factory workers, the machine operators, the assemblers, the warehouse workers. In service businesses, the workers behind the scenes are similarly overlooked.

Management people who distance themselves from this area of the business, consciously or subconsciously, are missing important opportunities for competitive advantage. At the same time, they are increasing the likelihood of quality problems and employee disaffection. In the 1970s and early 1980s, some attempts were made to involve employees by means of "quality circles," teams of employees that shared the same work function and met once a week, typically for an hour or so, to identify and correct problems. It was a copycat idea borrowed from the Japanese, usually with a disregard for the cultural differences between the United States and Japan.

The practice has largely disappeared. There were two problems. For the process to work well, a skilled facilitator was needed to run the meetings, and in most cases none was available. When the labor hours involved came under scrutiny, management was hard pressed to see the financial benefit. There were no measurements available to prove the value.

Quality improvement teams came next. The idea is to assemble a group of employees to pursue the solution of a specified problem. Usually management decides the problems to receive this kind of attention. Efficiency, cost, and productivity issues often are the instigator, although occasionally employees identify the problem and seek approval to take time to pursue a solution. But soon, management realized that more was needed than the ad hoc approach of quality improvement teams. The result came to be known as total quality management (TQM), a concept that involves all employees in improving the products and the processes of an organization. Product is defined as "what you pass on to another person." Process is the method used in performing work.

The problem with TQM is that there is no standardized approach or methodology. Consultants by the thousands define their own methods, think up clever names for their programs, copyright their materials, and try to convince clients that their approach is best. Clients soon find that cookie-cutter programs don't suit their unique environment. They begin customizing their own programs.

Into this chaotic arena stepped two combatants: the U.S. Department of Commerce, which created the Malcolm Baldrige National Quality Award, and the Geneva-based International Organization for Standards, which established ISO 9000. In the beginning, quality experts tended to take sides, favoring either Baldrige or ISO 9000. Now it is recognized that they are different and that each plays a significant role. (See Appendixes G and H for details.)

Baldrige emphasizes two core values that are at the heart of customer satisfaction. The Baldrige criteria state that "(1) Quality is judged by customers. All product and service characteristics that contribute value to customers and lead to customer satisfaction and preference must be a key focus of a company's management system. (2) Management by fact. A modern business management system needs to be built upon a framework of measurement, information, data, and analysis."[1]

Whereas Baldrige criteria spell out what must be done to achieve a high level of quality, the criteria do not specify how it should be done. That is left to each organization to decide for itself. ISO 9000 focuses on a think-through and documentation of every step in the processes needed to do business. After a rigorous audit, companies are certified. An exhaustive recertification audit is required periodically. ISO 9000 recognizes the importance of customer satisfaction but places much less emphasis on it.

It is important to understand that neither Baldrige nor ISO 9000 provides any guarantee that the organizations embracing them produce quality products and services. They simply establish a framework in which quality is most likely to be achieved.

# Life in the Trenches Hasn't Changed Much

Despite the emphasis that has been placed on quality in recent years, and the evolution in understanding what it takes to achieve continuous improvement, life for workers in the trenches often has not changed much. They show up, punch a time clock, do what they are told, and go home. Their opinions are rarely sought, and not much appreciated when offered.

Usually the closest they come to seeing customers is when management ("the suits") comes by, leading a gaggle of rubber-neckers. The workers are not introduced or acknowledged by name. They are supposed to look busy. It is not uncommon for workers to have no idea what happens to the work they do after it leaves their hands. In some cases, they have only the vaguest idea of who uses their products and how. It is dehumanizing.

This is not always the case. Consultant Chip Bell writes in the *At Work* newsletter about an experience his wife, a high-school principal, had when she ordered Valentine's Day ribbon bookmarkers for each member of her faculty. When the ribbons arrived, they were accompanied by a letter:

> Dear Dr. Bell:
> Thank you for ordering gold-stamped ribbons from Award Company of America. I am the machine operator who actually made your ribbons. I am very proud of my work. My company and I guarantee the ribbons to be to your complete satisfaction.
> We want to give you personal service. If you are dissatisfied for any reason, please contact our Customer Service department. They will contact me and I will personally correct any problem.
> Thank you again for your order. We all look forward to receiving your next order.
> Sincerely,
> Susan _____, Ribbon Machine Operator[2]

The simple device of a letter provides a connection between Susan and her customers. How much better it is than the familiar little slip of paper saying "This product was inspected by #6."

Involving workers in customer satisfaction can take several forms:

- Conduct periodic meetings to present the results of customer satisfaction measurement. Explain what the data, charts, and graphs mean as they relate to the work of the people on the line. Invite discussion and ideas. Report back on actions taken as a result of such meetings.

- Adopt the Baldrige Award criteria as a model, and involve production workers in a training program that explains Baldrige, including the rigorous requirements directed toward customer satisfaction.
- Invite customers in specifically to meet with groups of production workers. Ask customers to explain how they use the company's products or services. Invite their suggestions and ideas on how the customer relationship can be improved.
- Organize visits for groups of employees to customer locations and facilities, emphasizing the partnership nature of the relationship and encouraging discussions about how the relationship could be improved.
- Invite suppliers in to meet with groups of production workers to share ideas on how they can do a better job of satisfying customers together.
- Create an employee suggestion system program that really works, encouraging suggestions aimed at improving customer satisfaction.

# Paper Shuffling and Incomplete Ideas

Robert A. Schwarz, president of Total Quality Systems in Minneapolis, specializes in computer-based suggestion systems. He says the suggestion system is the most misunderstood process in industry because too many top management people remember the suggestion box of years ago that collected gum wrappers and was seldom serviced, and the suggestions went unanswered.

"Later," Schwarz asserts, "the process became one of massive amounts of paper being shuffled with ideas that were frequently half complete. The result was little support for the process, and the administrator needed a lot of skill to keep the process going. The persons responsible for evaluating were rarely allowed time for evaluations, and frequently were ridiculed by their supervisors for not having done the job right the first time."[3]

Cheap and powerful computing power, in the hands of enlightened managers, has changed all that. (A seven-step process for installing an effective suggestion system is in Appendix I.) Now, according to Schwartz:

- Suggestion system managers can easily prove that the systems are profit-generating processes.
- Data for each manager and executive can be sorted to minimize paper needed to evaluate the program.
- Data on the status of each suggestion can be accessible from many computer terminals.
- Performance of evaluators can be ranked based on elapsed days, time spent, savings created, etc.
- Performance of employees can be rated on numbers of ideas and savings created.
- Support for the Baldrige award is provided.[4]

Managers who decide to involve behind-the-scenes workers in customer satisfaction should recognize that it will come as something of a shock. People accustomed to being ignored—people who believe they are expected to check their brains at the door—are likely to be suspicious when management starts paying attention to them. Reactions can range from distrust and fear to confusion, anger, and disorientation. Any activity that even hints of change brings with it the unknown, and that in turn breeds anxiety. Some people may suffer a loss of self-esteem, feeling that what they did in the past was wrong and somehow their fault. The negative, nay-sayer types may seize the opportunity to find fault with everything the company does. Managers often have a tough time with this kind of attitude. Here they are, trying to make life better for everyone, and all they get is criticism.

The antidote for all of the emotions that can be aroused is communication, communication, communication. It is important to remember that communication is a two-way process involving at least as much listening as talking. Empathic listening does not necessarily come naturally to supervisors accustomed to making snap decisions and issuing peremptory orders. Listening training should be considered.

After all of the communicating, both listening and explaining, there will undoubtedly come a time when it is necessary to focus on the fact that the company was formed for the satisfaction of the customer, not the convenience of the worker. It is better to help employees arrive at this conclusion themselves than to lecture them on it.

Of course, employee attitudes reflect the way management is perceived. If employees see the company as existing for the benefit of management, and if this is constantly reinforced by the behaviors of management, it may be an uphill struggle to get employees to believe that the customer really comes first.

# Commitment to a Long-Term Process

To shift the way workers think about their jobs can take a long time. Managers shouldn't even start the process unless they are committed to a long-term process. As creatures of habit, we all change slowly, sometimes painfully. Psychologists point out the importance of reinforcing every move that employees make in the right direction. The message to leaders is to reinforce progress toward outcomes. Don't expect overnight change.

Americans traditionally want fast action and fast results. When quality programs first burst on the scene, they were expected to take hold and change everything in a matter of months. When that didn't happen, the time frame was extended to years. Now it is not uncommon to hear executives talk about programs expected to take decades.

The vice president in charge of quality for a multibillion-dollar corporation reflected wistfully that after fifteen years of intensive work on cultural change there was the possibility that "in two or three more years we could actually be the kind of company we want to be." Rather than focusing on programs, a better way to look at customer satisfaction is as a process of continuous improvement, with a beginning but no end. It is not a program, but a new way of life, a new attitude about what makes the organization tick.

# References

1. The Baldrige Criteria, p. 2, 3.
2. Chip Bell, "Dramatic Listening: Key to Customer Partnership," *At Work* (July / August 1994), p. 3.
3. Robert A. Schwarz, *Simplified Idea Management* (Maple Grove, Minn.: G & R Publishing, 1994).

# Appendixes

# Appendix A
# Deming's Fourteen Points

In 1986, W. Edwards Deming, in *Out of the Crisis* (published by the Massachusetts Institute of Technology Center for Advanced Engineering Study), listed his now famous Fourteen Points and Seven Deadly Diseases.

### The Fourteen Points

1. *Create constancy of purpose for improvement of product and service.* Deming's definition of a company's role: Rather than to make money, it is to stay in business and provide jobs through innovation, research, constant improvement, and maintenance.
2. *Adopt the new philosophy.* Americans are too tolerant of poor workmanship and sullen service. We need a new religion in which mistakes and negativism are unacceptable.
3. *Cease dependence on mass inspection.* American firms typically inspect a product as it comes off the assembly line or at major stages along the way; defective products are either thrown out or reworked. Both practices are unnecessarily expensive. In effect, a company is paying workers to make defects and then to correct them. Quality comes not from inspection but from

*Note:* This is excerpted from Mary Walton, *Deming Management at Work* (New York: G. P. Putnam, 1990).

improvement of the process. With instruction, workers can be enlisted in this improvement.

4. *End the practice of awarding business on the price tag alone.* Purchasing departments customarily operate on orders to seek the lowest-priced vendor. Frequently, this leads to supplies of low quality. Instead, buyers should seek the best quality in a long-term relationship with a single supplier for any one item.

5. *Improve constantly and forever the system of production and service.* Improvement is not a one-time effort. Management is obligated to continually look for ways to reduce waste and improve quality.

6. *Institute training.* Too often, workers have learned their job from another worker who was never trained properly. They are forced to follow unintelligible instructions. They can't do their jobs well because no one tells them how to do so.

7. *Institute leadership.* The job of a supervisor is not to tell people what to do, nor to punish them, but to lead. Leading consists of helping people do a better job, and of learning by objective methods who is in need of individual help.

8. *Drive out fear.* Many employees are afraid to ask questions or to take a position, even when they do not understand what their job is or what is right or wrong. They will continue to do things the wrong way, or not do them at all. The economic losses from fear are appalling. To assure better quality and productivity, it is necessary that people feel secure.

9. *Break down barriers between staff areas.* Often a company's departments or units are competing with each other or have goals that conflict. They do not work as a team so they can solve or foresee problems. Worse, one department's goals may cause trouble for another.

10. *Eliminate slogans, exhortations, and targets for the workforce.* These never helped anybody do a good job. Let workers formulate their own slogans.

11. *Eliminate numerical quotas.* Quotas take into account only numbers, not quality or methods. They are usually a guarantee of inefficiency and high cost. A person, to hold a job, meets a quota at any cost, without regard to damage to his company.

12. *Remove barriers to pride of workmanship.* People are eager to do a good job and distressed when they cannot. Too often, misguided supervisors, faulty equipment, and defective materials stand in the way of good performance. These barriers must be removed.

13. *Institute a vigorous program of education and retraining.* Both management and the work force have to be educated in the new methods, including teamwork and statistical techniques.
14. *Take action to accomplish the transformation.* It will require a special top management team with a plan of action to carry out the quality mission. Workers cannot do it on their own, nor can managers. A critical mass of people in the company must understand the Fourteen Points and the Seven Deadly Diseases.

# Appendix B
# Deming's Seven Deadly Diseases

In 1986, W. Edwards Deming, in *Out of the Crisis* (published by the Massachusetts Institute of Technology Center for Advanced Engineering Study), listed his now famous Fourteen Points and Seven Deadly Diseases.

### The Seven Deadly Diseases

1. *Lack of constancy of purpose.* A company that is without constancy of purpose has no long-range plans for staying in business. Management is insecure, and so are employees.
2. *Emphasis on short-term profits.* Looking to increase the quarterly dividend undermines quality and productivity.
3. *Evaluation by performance, merit rating, or annual review of performance.* The effects of these are devastating—teamwork is destroyed, rivalry is nurtured. Performance ratings build fear and leave people bitter, despondent, beaten. They also encourage defection in the ranks of management.
4. *Mobility of management.* Job-hopping managers never understand the companies they work for and are never there long enough to follow through on long-term changes that are necessary for quality and productivity.

*Note:* This is excerpted from Mary Walton, *Deming Management at Work* (New York: G. P. Putnam, 1990).

5. *Running a company on visible figures alone.* The most important figures are unknown and unknowable—the "multiplier" effect of a happy customer, for example.
6. *Excessive medical costs for employee health care, which increase the final costs of goods and services.*
7. *Excessive costs of warranty, fueled by lawyers who work on the basis of contingency fees.*

# *Appendix C*

# Customer Satisfaction Measurement: All-Employee Survey Questionnaire

## About Your Job

1. Do you serve customers directly or is your customer some-
   one else in the company?
   ☐ Serve customers directly
   ☐ Serve internal customers
   ☐ Don't know    ☐ No effect on any customers
2. Do you think your job has an effect on how satisfied cus-
   tomers are about doing business with your company?
   ☐ Very much so    ☐ Somewhat    ☐ Not sure    ☐ No

*Source:* Customer Inc., Minneapolis, Minn.

3. Are there any measurements of customer satisfaction that relate to your job?
☐ Yes     ☐ No     ☐ Don't know
4. I think it is a good idea to pay people more for doing a good job of satisfying customers, based on reliable and fair measurement methods.
☐ Agree strongly     ☐ Agree     ☐ Not sure
☐ Disagree     ☐ Disagree strongly

# About the Company

5. In general do you think your company puts the customer first?
☐ Yes     ☐ No     ☐ Somewhat
6. There are many forces driving companies, but usually one predominates. Please check the force that you believe dominates in your company.
☐ Sales                     ☐ Profits          ☐ Competition
☐ Growth                    ☐ Marketing        ☐ Product
☐ Customer satisfaction     ☐ Tradition        ☐ Cash flow
☐ Stockholder value         ☐ Vision           ☐ Strategic plan
☐ Other (please specify) _____

7. How do you think your company would rank on a Customer Satisfaction Measurement survey?
☐ Very satisfied     ☐ Somewhat satisfied
☐ Neither satisfied nor dissatisfied
☐ Somewhat dissatisfied     ☐ Very dissatisfied
8. Over the past year, do you think your company has done better or worse in the area of Customer Satisfaction?
☐ Much better     ☐ Better     ☐ About the same
☐ Worse     ☐ Much worse

# About Management

9. Top management is always committed to having a company that is truly customer driven.
☐ Agree strongly     ☐ Agree     ☐ Not sure
☐ Disagree     ☐ Disagree strongly

10. The top people believe in Customer Satisfaction Measurement and make sure that information is displayed for all to see.
☐ Agree strongly    ☐ Agree    ☐ Not sure
☐ Disagree    ☐ Disagree strongly

11. Management asks " What is best for the customer?" and believes in making decisions based on Customer Satisfaction Measurement findings.
☐ Agree strongly    ☐ Agree    ☐ Not sure
☐ Disagree    ☐ Disagree strongly

# What Do You Think?

12. There is a strong commitment to *product quality* in our company.
☐ Agree strongly    ☐ Agree    ☐ Not sure
☐ Disagree    ☐ Disagree strongly

13. There is a strong commitment to quality in all aspects of *customer relationships* in addition to product. For example, service, delivery, billing, literature.
☐ Agree strongly    ☐ Agree    ☐ Not sure
☐ Disagree    ☐ Disagree strongly

14. The customer is the ultimate judge of quality and in the end will determine whether we are successful or not.
☐ Agree strongly    ☐ Agree    ☐ Not sure
☐ Disagree    ☐ Disagree strongly

15. I have a suggestion *related to my job* about something we could do to improve customer satisfaction. Here it is: _____
_____
_____
_____

16. I have a suggestion for *the company in general* about something we could do to improve customer satisfaction. Here it is _____
_____
_____
_____

17. Other comments _____
_____
_____
_____

# Appendix D

# Customer Satisfaction Measurement: Frontline Employee Questionnaire

1. Many factors affect the way customers make decisions and their degree of loyalty. What characteristics about your product and services do you feel may be important to your customers?
2. Have you determined, relatively speaking, which of these characteristics are *the most important?*
3. Customers have certain expectations of performance concern-

*Source:* Customer Inc., Minneapolis, Minn.

ing key characteristics. Have you determined what are the minimum performance levels to satisfy your customer's requirements?

4. Tell me about the way you keep track of your customer contacts. What do you record? What kind of forms do you use?

5. Do you use your customer contacts as an opportunity to ask customers what they think about the company and its products and services?

6. Based on your experience with customers, what do you think would be the results of a customer satisfaction survey? Very satisfied, satisfied, dissatisfied, very dissatisfied.

7. Is customer satisfaction measurement something that gets discussed very often?

8. Is there anything you think the company should be doing to improve customer satisfaction?

9. What do you think customers like best about your company?

10. As far as you know, what is the most frequently heard complaint from customers?

11. Compared to competitors, do you think your company is doing better, worse, or about the same?

12. Do you feel the management of the company is committed to putting the customer first?

13. Do you feel your fellow workers believe the customer should come first and are willing to go out of their way for them?

14. Are there any measurements in place that accurately reflect how well you are doing your job?

15. Have you had any customer service training? If so, how would you rate it?

16. If you were given the opportunity to change one thing about your job, what would it be?

17. Does the company pay attention to suggestions from employees? Have you ever made any suggestions, and, if so, how did you feel about the way they were received?

18. Some companies are paying their people based on customer satisfaction measurement scores. Do you think that is fair?

19. Have you noticed any changes recently in the attitude of customers toward the company? If so, what were they?

20. How would you describe the morale in the company?

21. There is a lot of talk about how fast things are changing in today's world and the pressures of competition. Are these things you feel in your job?

22. In your judgment, what is the driving force of this company?

Profits, growth, customer satisfaction, shareholder value, competitive pressure, strategic planning, tradition, or something else?

23. Would you say this is a company committed to quality in every aspect of the way it does business?

24. If you became president of this company, what is the first change you would make?

# *Appendix E*

# Customer Satisfaction Measurement: Executive Questionnaire

1. Many factors affect the way customers make decisions and their degree of loyalty. What characteristics about your product and service do you feel may be important to your customers?
2. Have you determined, relatively speaking, which characteristics are the *most* important?
3. Customers have certain expectations of performance concerning these key characteristics. Have you determined what are minimum performance levels to satisfy your customers' requirements?

*Source:* Customer Inc., Minneapolis, Minn.

4. What kind of information do you have about your customers?
5. How is this information gathered?
6. Do you have a method for segmentation analysis of your total customer base, e.g., best customers vs. occasional customers?
7. What kind of continuing listening strategies do you use to validate what you know about important product and service characteristics?
8. Are you continuously planning to improve your process for keeping track of what's important to your customers? If so, please describe.
9. How much do you know about your competitor's customers?
10. The competitive environment is always changing. What methods do you use to monitor this situation?
11. How do customers request information and get assistance from you?
12. Do you have a system for tracking requests for information?
13. Are there systems in place that make it easy for customers to complain? If so, please describe.
14. Please tell us about your complaint management process, including the steps you take to eliminate the causes of complaints.
15. Are results posted?
16. What methods do you employ for following up with customers to find out whether they are satisfied with products or services, and to solicit suggestions?
17. Do you have measurable standards for customer response activities such as complaint resolution time, order processing, providing answers to queries, number of rings before phone is answered? How frequently are they reviewed? How do they compare to competitors?
18. What methods do you use to determine customer satisfaction?
    a. If appropriate, the Sources of Customer Satisfaction Information Questionnaire is completed at this point.
19. Do you have ways of finding out how your customer satisfaction levels compare to your competitors?
20. Are you able to link your customer satisfaction data directly to your key business processes?
21. Are you able to determine the cost/revenue implications of your customer satisfaction data?
22. Does your measurement data pinpoint both satisfiers and dissatisfiers?

23. Before measurement data can attain their full potential for usefulness, they have to be gathered in ways that clearly show trends. What kind of trend data do you have?

24. Do you have or could you easily produce a flow chart showing how customer satisfaction measurement data are collected, communicated throughout the organization, and acted upon?

25. Do you have processes and methods for integrating and cross-checking customer satisfaction measurement data from many different sources?

26. Do you link customer satisfaction measurement and compensation in your organization? If so, at what levels and how?

27. Do you gather data on internal customers with the same customer satisfaction objectives as you have for external customers?

28. Do you use customer satisfaction measurement data as a driver for your management and employee training and development programs?

29. Are you familiar with and have you considered using the Malcolm Baldrige Award guidelines as a way of evaluating your customer satisfaction measurement programs?

30. How do you think your employees would rate your personal commitment to customer satisfaction on a scale of 1 to 10, with 10 being the most committed?

31. There is a predominant driving force for every business. Examples: growth, new products, profits, customer satisfaction, shareholder value, cost, service, innovation, R&D, tradition. What do you consider the real driving force to be in your business?

32. As important as what people say is what they actually do—their market behaviors. Do you track this with data on frequency of purchase, repurchase, complaints, positive referrals, new business?

33. What data do you have on gains and losses of customers and customer accounts relative to competitors?

34. What data do you have on gains and losses in market share?

35. Are you able to establish linkages between the data called for in questions 32, 33, 34, and your policies, products, and customer service performance?

36. Do you think most people in the company would give the same answer you just did?

# Appendix F
# Auto Industry Surveys

The American auto industry has been using surveys since 1978 to help dealers measure their performance against other dealers in order to identify operations that needed improvement. In some cases, the surveys have become unwieldy one-hundred-question documents.

The National Automobile Dealers Association intervened in 1994 with a much shorter recommended approach to determining a Customer Satisfaction Index (CSI). The entire survey uses only the following eight issues:

1. My vehicle was clean and ready to go.
2. My salesperson was courteous and professional.
3. The business/finance department handled the sales transaction professionally.
4. The warranty and maintenance schedules were explained to me.
5. The owner's manual and operating controls were properly explained to me.
6. Overall, I am pleased with my new vehicle.
7. Overall, I am pleased with the way my new vehicle was sold and delivered to me.
8. Overall, I would recommend (name of dealership) to my friends.

A similarly brief and to-the-point service questionnaire was recommended, with these seven issues:

1. It was easy to get my service appointment.
2. Our repairs were properly explained.
3. The vehicle was ready when promised.
4. The vehicle was repaired properly.
5. Our service fees were fair.
6. Overall, I am pleased with my service experience.
7. Overall, I would recommend the dealership to friends for service work.

# Appendix G

# Malcolm Baldrige National Quality Award Criteria

## Core Values and Concepts

The award criteria are built upon a set of core values and concepts, which are excerpted here as they relate to customer satisfaction. These values and concepts are the foundation for integrating customer and company performance requirements.

### Customer-Driven Quality

Quality is judged by customers. All product and service characteristics that contribute value to customers and lead to customer satisfaction and preference must be a key focus of a company's management system. Value, satisfaction, and preference may be influenced by many factors throughout the customer's overall purchase, ownership, and service experiences. These factors include the company's relationship with customers that helps build trust, confidence, and loyalty. This concept of quality includes not only the product and service characteristics that meet basic customer requirements, but it also includes those characteristics that enhance them and differentiate them from competing offerings. Such enhancement and differentiation may be based upon new offerings, combinations of product and service offerings, rapid response, or special relationships.

Customer-driven quality is thus a strategic concept. It is directed toward customer retention and market share gain. It demands constant sensitivity to emerging customer and market requirements, and measurement of the factors that drive customer satisfaction and retention. It also demands awareness of developments in technology and of competitors' offerings, and rapid and flexible response to customer and market requirements.

Success requires more than defect and error reduction, merely meeting specifications, and reducing complaints. Nevertheless, defect and error reduction and elimination of causes of dissatisfaction contribute significantly to the customers' view of quality and are thus also important parts of customer-driven quality. In addition, the company's success in recovering from defects and errors is crucial to building customer relationships and to customer retention.

## Leadership

A company's senior leaders need to set directions and create a customer orientation, clear and visible values, and high expectations. Reinforcement of the values and expectations requires personal commitment and involvement. The leaders' basic values and commitment need to include areas of public responsibility and corporate citizenship. The leaders need to take part in the creation of strategies, systems, and methods for achieving excellence and building capabilities. The senior leaders need to commit to the development of the entire workforce and should encourage participation and creativity by all employees.

## Continuous Improvement and Learning

Achieving the highest levels of performance requires a well-executed approach to continuous improvement. The term *continuous improvement* refers to both incremental and "breakthrough" improvement. Opportunities for improvement include employee ideas, R&D, customer input, and benchmarking or other comparative performance information.

Improvements may be of several types: (1) enhancing value to customers through new and improved products and services; (2) reducing errors, defects, and waste; (3) improving responsiveness and cycle time performance; (4) improving productivity and effectiveness in the use of all resources; and (5) improving the company's performance and leadership position in fulfilling its public responsibilities and serving as a role model in corporate citizenship.

## Employee Participation and Development

A company's success in improving performance depends increasingly on the skills and motivation of its workforce. Employee success depends increasingly on having meaningful opportunities to learn and to practice new skills. Companies need to invest in the development of the workforce through ongoing education, training, and opportunities for continuing growth.

Addressing these challenges requires acquisition and use of employee-related data on skills, satisfaction, motivation, safety, and well-being. Such data need to be tied to indicators of company or unit performance, such as customer satisfaction, customer retention, and productivity.

## Fast Response

Success in competitive markets increasingly demands ever-shorter cycles for new or improved product and service introduction. Also, faster and more flexible response to customers is now a more critical requirement. Major improvement in response time often requires simplification of work organizations and work processes. To accomplish such improvement, the time performance of work processes should be among the key process measures.

## Design Quality and Prevention

Business management should place strong emphasis on design quality—problem and waste prevention achieved through building quality into products and services and into production and delivery processes.

## Long-Range View of the Future

Pursuit of market leadership requires a strong future orientation and a willingness to make long-term commitments to all stakeholders: customers, employees, suppliers, stockholders, the public, and the community. Planning needs to anticipate many types of changes, including those that may affect customers' expectations of product and services, technological developments, changing customer segments, evolving regulatory requirements, community/societal expectations, and thrusts by competitors.

## Management by Fact

A modern business management system needs to be built upon a framework of measurements, information, data, and analysis. Measurements must derive from the company's strategy and encompass all key processes and the outputs and results of those processes. Facts and data needed for performance improvement and assessment are of many types, including customer, product and service performance, operations, market, competitive comparisons, suppliers, employee-related, and cost and financial. The measures or indicators should be selected to best represent the factors that lead to improved customer, operational, and financial performance. A system of measures or indicators tied to customer and/or company performance requirements represents a clear and objective basis for aligning all activities with the company's goals. Measures selected to track product and service quality may be judged by how well improvement in these measures correlates with improvement in customer satisfaction and customer retention.

## Partnership Development

Companies should seek to build internal and external partnerships to better accomplish their overall goals. Internal partnerships might include those that promote labor-management cooperation, such as agreements with unions. Agreements might entail employee development, cross-training, or new work organizations, such as high-performance work teams. External partnerships may be with customers, suppliers, and education organizations for a variety of purposes, including education and training.

## Corporate Responsibility and Citizenship

A company's management should stress corporate responsibility and citizenship. Corporate responsibility refers to basic expectations of the company—business ethics and protection of public health, safety, and the environment. Health, safety, and environment considerations need to take into account the company's operations as well as the life cycles of products and services.

## Results Orientation

A company's performance system needs to focus on results. Results ought to be guided by and balanced by the interests of all stakeholders: customers, employees, stockholders, suppliers and partners, the public, and the community. To meet the sometimes conflicting and changing aims that balance implies, company strategy needs to explicitly address all stakeholder requirements to ensure that actions and plans meet the differing needs and avoid adverse impact on the stakeholders. The use of a balanced composite of performance indicators offers an effective means to communicate requirements, to monitor actual performance, and to marshal support for improving results.

# Baldrige Award Criteria Framework

The core values and concepts are embodied in seven categories, as follows: (1) Leadership, (2) Information and Analysis, (3) Strategic Planning, (4) Human Resource Development and Management, (5) Process Management, (6) Business Results, and (7) Customer Focus and Satisfaction.

## Customer Focus and Satisfaction

Customer Focus and Satisfaction (Category 7) is the focal point within the Criteria for understanding in detail the voices of customers and the marketplace. Much of the information needed for this understanding comes from measuring results and trends. Such results and trends provide hard information on customers' views and their marketplace behaviors. This provides a useful foundation for setting priorities and focusing improvement activities. The results and trends offer a means to determine whether or not priorities and improvement activities are appropriately directed.

### 7.1 Customer and Market Knowledge

This item addresses how the company determines current and emerging customer requirements and expectations. The thrust of the item is that many factors may affect customer preference and customer loyalty, making it necessary to listen and learn on a continuous basis.

Area 7.1a calls for information on the company's process for determining current and near-term requirements and expectations of customers. The information sought concerns the completeness of the customer pool, including recognition of segments and customers of competitors. Other information sought relates to sensitivity to specific product and service requirements and their relative importance to customer groups. The Area is concerned with overall validity of determination methods. The validity should be backed by use of other data and information such as complaints and gains and losses of customers.

Area 7.1b calls for information on how the company addresses future requirements and expectations of customers—its key listening and learning strategies. Such strategies depend a great deal upon the nature of the company's products and services, the competitive environment, and relationships with customers. The listening and learning strategy selected should provide timely and useful information for decision making. The strategy should take into account the company's competitive strategy. For example, if the company customizes its products and services, the listening and learning strategy needs to be backed by a capable information system—one that rapidly accumulates information about customers and makes this information available where needed throughout the company.

Area 7.1c calls for information on how the company evaluates and improves its processes for determining customer requirements and expectations. Such evaluation/improvement could entail a variety of approaches—formal and informal—that seek to stay in close touch with customers and with issues that bear upon customer loyalty and customer preference. The purpose of the evaluation called for in Area 7.1c is to find reliable and cost-effective means to understand customer requirements and expectations on a continuous basis.

## 7.2 Customer Relationship Management

Item 7.2 addresses how the company provides effective management of its responses and follow-ups with customers. Relationship management provides a potentially important means for companies to gain understanding about, and to manage, customer expectations. Also, frontline employees may provide vital information relating to building partnerships and other long-term relationships with customers.

Area 7.2a calls for information on how the company provides easy access for customers, specifically for purposes of seeking information on assistance and/or to comment and complain. This Area also calls for information on service standards and their use.

Area 7.2b focuses on the complaint management process. The principal issue addressed is prompt and effective resolution of complaints including recovery of customer confidence. However, the Area also addresses how the company learns from complaints and ensures that product/delivery process employees receive information needed to eliminate the causes of complaints.

Area 7.2c calls for information on how the company follows up with customers regarding products, services, and recent transactions to determine satisfaction, to resolve problems, and to gather information for improvement or for new services.

Area 7.2d calls for information on how the company evaluates and improves its customer response management. Such improvements may be of several types. Examples include improvement of service standards, such as complaint resolution time and resolution effectiveness, and improving the use of customer feedback to improve product/delivery processes, training, and hiring.

## 7.3 Customer Satisfaction Determination

This item addresses how the company determines customer satisfaction and satisfaction relative to competitors.

Area 7.3a calls for information on how the company gathers information on customer satisfaction, including any important differences in approaches for different customer groups or segments. The Area highlights the importance of the measurement of sales to focus on the factors that reflect customers' market behaviors: repurchase, new business, and positive referral.

Area 7.3b calls for information on how satisfaction relative to competitors is determined. Such information might be derived from company-based comparative studies or studies made by independent organizations. The purpose of this comparison is to develop information that can be used for improving performance relative to competitors and to better understand the factors that drive markets.

Area 7.3c calls for information on how the company evaluates and improves its processes and measurement scales for determining customer satisfaction and satisfaction relative to competitors. This evaluation/improvement process is expected to draw upon other indicators such as gains and losses of customers and customer dissatisfaction indicators such as complaints. The evaluation should also consider how well customer satisfaction information and data are used throughout the company. Such use is likely to be enhanced if data are presented in an actionable form meeting two key conditions: (1) survey responses tying directly to key business processes, and (2) survey responses translated into cost/revenue implications.

## 7.4 Customer Satisfaction Results

This item addresses two related but nevertheless different types of business results: customer satisfaction and customer dissatisfaction.

Area 7.4a calls for information on trends and current levels in key measures and/or indicators of customer satisfaction. The presentation of results could include information on customer retention and other appropriate evidence of current and recent past satisfaction with the company's products and/or services, such as customer awards.

Area 7.4b calls for trends in key measures and/or indicators of customer dissatisfaction. Such measures and/or indicators depend upon the nature of the products and/or services. Item 7.3, Note (3), lists a number of possible indicators of dissatisfaction. In addition, a company's survey methods might include a scale that uses ratings such as "very dissatisfied" or "somewhat dissatisfied."

The reason for including measures of both satisfaction and dissatisfaction is that they usually provide different information. That is, the factors in high levels of satisfaction may not be the same factors as those that relate to high levels of dissatisfaction. In addition, the effect of individual instances of dissatisfaction on overall satisfaction could vary widely depending upon the effectiveness of the company's resolution ("recovery") of a problem.

Although Item 7.4 is a results item, it is anticipated that the results themselves are *input* drivers of improvement priorities—actions that affect customer retention and positive referral. That is, the main management approach involves viewing increasing satisfaction and decreasing dissatisfaction as a means, not an end. The end is retention and positive referral. Use of customer satisfaction data and information is called for in Item 2.3.

## 7.5 Customer Satisfaction Comparison

This item addresses three related but nevertheless different customer-related results, important to managing in a competitive environment. These are customer satisfaction relative to competitors, gains and losses of customers and customer accounts relative to competitors, and gains and losses in market share.

Area 7.5a calls for information on trends and current levels in key measures and/or indicators of customer satisfaction relative to competitors. The presentation of results could include information on gains and losses of customers and customer accounts relative to competitors.

Area 7.5b calls for trends in gaining or losing market share to competitors.

The reason for including the three measures is that they provide different information. Relative satisfaction and gains and losses of customers and customer accounts provide information on specific factors and the importance of these factors in customer decision making. Market share information provides a more aggregate view of markets that includes but goes beyond customer turnover.

Although Item 7.5 is a results item, it is anticipated that the results themselves are drivers of improvement priorities and market understanding, reinforcing but going beyond the information presented in Item 7.5. Use of customer satisfaction comparison data and information is called for in Item 2.3.

# Appendix H

# ISO 9000: Meeting Customer Expectations and Requirements

ISO 9000 is the offspring of the International Organization for Standardization (ISO). Based in Geneva, Switzerland, ISO is a consortium of virtually all the world's industrialized nations—from Albania to Zimbabwe. The group's mission is to develop industrial standards that facilitate international trade. The United States is represented on ISO by the American National Standards Institute (ANSI), a very familiar name in American industry.

ISO 9000 is not a product standard, but a *quality system standard*. It applies not to products or services, but to the process which creates them. It is designed and intended to apply to virtually any product or service made by any process anywhere in the world.

*Source:* The description of ISO 9000 and how it is applied is excerpted from ISO 9000 *Meeting the New International Standards* (McGraw-Hill, 1993) by Perry L. Johnson, founder and president of a consulting firm specializing in total quality management and ISO 9000 training and implementation.

To achieve this generic state, ISO 9000 refrains, to the greatest extent possible, from mandating specific methods, practices, and techniques. It emphasizes principle, goals, and objectives. All of these focus on one objective, the same objective which drives every business: *meeting customer expectations and requirements.*

A well-designed, well-implemented, and carefully managed ISO 9000 quality system provides confidence that the output of the process will meet customer expectations and requirements. It is aimed at providing that confidence to three audiences:

- The customers directly
- The customers indirectly (via third-party assessments and quality system registration)
- Company management and staff

ISO 9000 does so by requiring that every business activity affecting quality be conducted in a three-part, never-ending cycle: planning, control, and documentation.

- Activities affecting quality must be *planned* to ensure that goals, authority, and responsibility are defined and understood.
- Activities affecting quality must be *controlled* to ensure that specified requirements (at all levels) are met, problems are anticipated and averted, and corrective actions are planned and carried out.
- Activities affecting quality must be *documented* to ensure understanding of quality objectives and methods, smooth interaction within the organization, feedback for the planning cycle, and objective evidence of quality system performance for those who require it, such as customers or third-party assessors.

ISO 9000 is not new or radical. It is good, hardheaded, common business sense in codified, verifiable, and easily adapted form. It has strong commonalities with other quality schemes, such as MIL-Q, Deming's 14 points, total quality management, and the Malcolm Baldrige National Quality Award criteria.

The main difference is that a firm can *register* to ISO 9000.

There are two broad ways to apply the ISO 9000 quality system standard. One way is to implement it for *quality management purposes*—that is, to obtain its benefits for their own sake.

The other way is to obtain *certification* or, more properly, *registration* to the ISO 9000 quality system standard. Registration provides the benefits of quality system management, plus significant strategic advantages.

Registration is awarded by an accredited third-party registration body after it satisfies itself, by reviewing documentation and conducting on-site assessments (audits), that the firm's quality system conforms to the ISO 9000 standard. ISO 9000 registration is renewable, and enforced by semiannual surveillance visits by the registration body.

Conformance to ISO 9000 is almost impossible to *fake*. The standard focuses on performance, documentation, and objective evidence. There are no shortcuts.

# Appendix I

# Seven Steps to a Suggestion System

1. Top management must define the level of awards and team authority that they will support. This is essentially a sharing of wealth and power requiring approval and involvement of top management before the next steps are taken. Management must also identify the nature of the culture they envision. For example, what level of team process is desired and what problem solving training is planned?

2. Form a steering committee representing all levels of the organization. Train the committee by describing some of the best suggestion systems so they understand what is possible (external benchmarking). By understanding the options, they can effectively identify details of your new process.

3. Lead the committee through a process of expectations analysis. The committee members will identify what the expectations are for each of the suggestion functions. This is usually suggester, supervisor, evaluator, top management, and the system admin-

*Source:* Excerpted from *Simplified Idea Management* (G& R Publishing, 1994) by Robert A. Schwarz, president of Total Quality Systems in Minneapolis, Minnesota.

istrator/manager. These expectations are prioritized and shared with all employees to develop ownership. The expectations are then refined with the input from other employees.

4. The prioritized list of expectations are next structured into input to each of the five functions and output from each function. This input/output analysis defines the needs of each function and the resource.

5. Report requirements can easily be defined from the data in the input/output analysis. Report definitions must be precise as to the data needed, the distribution required, and the timing. Reports should be carefully designed to focus on only the information each recipient needs to take needed action to support the system. Personal computers allow effective sorting to meet each person's needs.

6. Software and suggestion forms must be designed to collect and process the raw data demanded by the report requirements. Other materials like posters, handbooks, and promotional materials must be created. It is important for the process to be effective so that all participants get what they need to do their job.

7. The system is defined and designed at this point. The implementation requires thorough training and the use of attention-getting and motivational materials to make the process exciting. Presentations and reporting to top management are vital to assure continued support.

# Recommended Reading

Block, Peter. *Stewardship*. San Francisco: Berrett-Koehler Publishers, 1993.

Drucker, Peter F. *Post-Capitalist Society*. New York: HarperCollins, 1993.

Hamel, Gary, and C. K. Prahalad. *Competing for the Future*. Boston: Harvard Business School Press, 1994.

Hammer, Michael, and James Champy. *Reengineering the Corporation*. New York: HarperCollins, 1993.

Handy, Charles. *The Age of Paradox*. Boston: Harvard Business School Press, 1994.

Imparato, Nicholas, and Oren Harari. *Jumping the Curve*. San Francisco: Jossey-Bass Publishers, 1994.

Jacobs, Robert W. *Real Time Strategic Change*. San Francisco: Berrett-Koehler Publishers, 1994.

Janov, Jill. *The Inventive Organization*. San Francisco: Jossey-Bass Publishers, 1994.

Joiner, Brian L. *Fourth Generation Management*. New York: McGraw-Hill, 1994.

Katzenbach, Jon R., and Douglas K. Smith. *The Wisdom of Teams*. New York: HarperCollins, 1993.

Kline, Peter, and Bernard Saunders. *Ten Steps to a Learning Organization*. Arlington, Va.: Great Ocean Publishers, 1993.

Kotter, John P. *Leading Change*. Boston: Harvard Business School Press, 1996.

Naumann, Earl. *Creating Customer Value*. Cincinnati, Ohio: Thomson Executive Press, 1995.

Naumann, Earl, and Kathleen Giel. *Customer Satisfaction Measurement and Management*. Cincinnati, Ohio: Thomson Executive Press, 1995.

Peppers, Don, and Martha Rogers. *The One to One Future*. New York: Doubleday, 1993.

Pinchot, Clifford and Elizabeth. *The End of Bureaucracy & The Rise of the Intelligent Organization*. San Francisco: Berrett-Koehler, 1993.

Rapp, Stan, and Thomas L. Collins. *Beyond Maxi-Marketing*. New York: McGraw-Hill, 1994.

Rosen, Robert H. *The Healthy Company*. New York: Putnam Publishing Group, 1992.

Schaaf, Dick. *Keeping the Edge*. New York: Dutton, 1995.

Senge, Peter M. *The Fifth Discipline,* New York: Doubleday, 1990.

Sewell, Carl, and Paul B. Brown. *Customers for Life*. New York: Doubleday, 1990.

Tichy, Noel M., and Stratford Sherman. *Control Your Destiny or Someone Else Will*. New York: Doubleday, 1993.

Tomasko, Robert M. *Rethinking the Corporation*. New York: AMACOM, 1993.

Walton, Mary. *Deming Management at Work*. New York: G.P. Putnam, 1990.

Whitely, Richard C. *The Customer Driven Company*. Reading, Mass.: Addison-Wesley, 1991.

Zeithaml, Valerie A., A. Parasuraman, and Leonard L. Berry. *Delivering Quality Service*. New York: The Free Press, 1990.

# Index